THE SNAKE'S ADVOCATE

by

ARTHUR CARL STIMSON

Honorary Curator of Reptiles
The Museum of Natural Science of Houston
and
The Houston Zoological Gardens

Edited and Compiled
by his daughter

DOROTHY E. JUSTMAN

Eakin Press

FIRST EDITION

Library of Congress Catalog Card Number: 82-72010
ISBN No.0-89015-355-8

TABLE OF CONTENTS

CHAPTER PAGE

I. Prevention of Snakebite 1
II. Identifying the Dangerous Snakes 6
III. Treatment of Snakebite 19
IV. Sizes and Feeding Habits 31
V. "Charming" 38
VI. Is the Spreading Adder a Remarkable Actor? 43
VII. The Milk Snake 48
VIII. The Hoop Snake 52
IX. The Sea Serpent 55
X. The Coachwhip 58
XI. Another Tarantula 61
XII. Tall Tales 65
XIII. The One That Got Away! 73
XIV. Fact Not Fiction 75
Addendum 83
Bibliography 96
Index 103

Arthur Carl Stimson
b. 8 Feb. 1892 d. 21 Jan. 1968

"I am in hopes that my research may be the nucleus around which may be built a less heroic method of snakebite treatment."

That Kind of Man

BY LOUIS HOFFERBERT

Once in a while you meet a person who has the knack of making you feel like an old friend in five minutes. It is a special sort of talent, and I don't know exactly what to call it. Maybe sincerity, maybe courtesy, maybe just natural friendliness that spills over on anybody handy. But whatever you call it, Arthur Stimson had it.

And it made me feel I lost an old friend when he died this week.

The truth is, I didn't know Mr. Stimson very well, though I knew him in a casual way for quite a while. Most of our talks were by phone, either me calling him with a question or him calling me to comment on something he saw or read. He was 75 years old and not in good health lately. But he was sharp as a tack and when he said something you knew it was worth hearing.

As a good many folks know, Arthur Stimson was one of this country's top experts on snakes. He was a surveyor and civil engineer by trade, same as his father. But his hobby was snakes, and I expect there were times when his family figured the hobby was bigger than the job.

Working so much outdoors, Mr. Stimson got a better first-hand knowledge of all kinds of East Texas wildlife than most folks. But he soon decided snakes were something people ought to know more about, for their own good and the snakes' good, too.

So he put in half a century learning about snakes and passing on what he learned. He wrote a great many scientific papers, headed the Museum of Natural History for a while, and swapped information with top-flight herpetologists all over the world.

In spite of all his knowledge, Mr. Stimson was modest to a fault. He never bragged, and he never tried to be impressive. He even acted like I knew about as much as he did, which is mighty nice to think about but a long way from being true.

It was my privilege to talk with him one time for several hours, sitting in a pleasant book-and paper-filled room of his home on Elmen. He showed me the manuscript of a book on snakes he wrote a few years ago, then decided not to publish. It was fascinating to me, and I hope it still can be published sometime.

There is no way to measure the help Arthur Stimson gave to people who were bitten by snakes. Nor the help he gave snakes by teaching people to know which ones are poisonous and which are harmless. He was a great respecter of dangerous snakes, but he was scornful of what he called snake myths and old wives' tales. A good part of his unpublished book debunks phony snake legends.

I would guess that dozens of people owe their lives, or their full recovery from snakebite, to the kindness, patience and knowledge of Arthur Stimson. And that hundreds of beneficial East Texas snakes owe their lives to the same thing. What's more, I have a feeling Mr. Stimson was as proud and happy over the second achievement as the first.

He was that kind of man.

____Quoted from Texas Notebook. *The Houston Chronicle, Jan. 25, 1968.*

Houston Lighting
& Power Company

ELECTRIC BUILDING, HOUSTON 1, TEXAS

July 14, 1959

Mr. A.C. Stimson
2119 Elmen
Houston, Texas

Dear Mr. Stimson:

I want to express my appreciation and that of the Houston Lighting & Power Company for your fine work in connection with the recent snakebite sustained by our Mr. G.B. Springer over the weekend.

Dr. Tucker has told me of the interest you took in the case and of your conscientious effort to be of all assistance possible. I am told you do this as a public service, and certainly you are to be commended for this fine spirit. It must give you a good deal of personal satisfaction to be able to be of such valuable assistance to your fellow man.

With best wishes,

Sincerely,

Carl B. Sherman
Vice President

CBS:rh

The Methodist Hospital

Jackson 9-3611

6516 Bertner Blvd.

Texas Medical Center

Houston 25, Texas

29 October 1960

Mr. A. C. Stimson
Honorary Curator of Reptiles
Museum of Natural History
2119 Elmen Street
Houston 19, Texas

Dear Mr. Stimson:

Just a note of gratitude for your reprints concerning the treatment of venomous animal poisoning, and particularly the article on the treatment of snakebite.

Your expert consultation, without pay, concerning venomous poisonings is a most generous service to this hospital and to the community.

Again, I wish to thank you for your comments and advice given in our telephone conversation yesterday, and for the fine articles.

Yours truly,

Ben Tobias
Assistant Administrator

n
11-4-60

PURPOSE

My sole purpose in editing and compiling this manuscript is to preserve my father's notes for posterity in order that his lifework on the treatment of snakebite should not die with him.

In a letter to Judge Wilmer Hunt, Carl Stimson wrote that he had experimented with rattlesnake venom and kingsnake's blood as far back as 1930 in an effort to produce a non-allergic serum. At the time of his death in 1968, he and Dr. E.J. Tucker were collaberating on experiments on rats, still in the hope of discovering a blood-based serum with less harmful allergic reactions.

Should the information in this book give any future doctors a clue as to "less heroic methods of snakebite treatment," my purpose as a catalyst would have been served.

"Debunking" snake myths was almost a phobia with Carl Stimson, especially those debasing the snakes. He had planned a book of these stories, to which he had given the title "Mostly of Snakes," but as I read his defense of snakes, I began to think of him as *The Snake's Advocate.*

As a memorial to Carl Stimson and out of gratitude to John E. Werler, any profit that may be made on this book will go to the reptile house of the Houston Zoological Gardens.

ACKNOWLEDGMENTS

Acknowledgments are made to the following:

J. LEWIS STIMSON

my half-brother,
who brought our father's original notes to me,
and to his mother,

IRENE GAWLEY STIMSON

patient, loving wife of A.C. Stimson,
who introduced me to her cousin,

RUTH HADDON WRIGHT

who persuaded her brother,

E.P. HADDON

to permit me to use original photographs from his article
"When a Rattlesnake Bites"
taken of his friend,

JOHN E. WERLER

Director of the Houston Zoological Gardens

who proof read, corrected, and up-dated the manuscript
as conscientiously and meticulously as he would have for
his lifelong friend and admirer,

ARTHUR CARL STIMSON

who kept a lifetime file of records and stories about snakes.

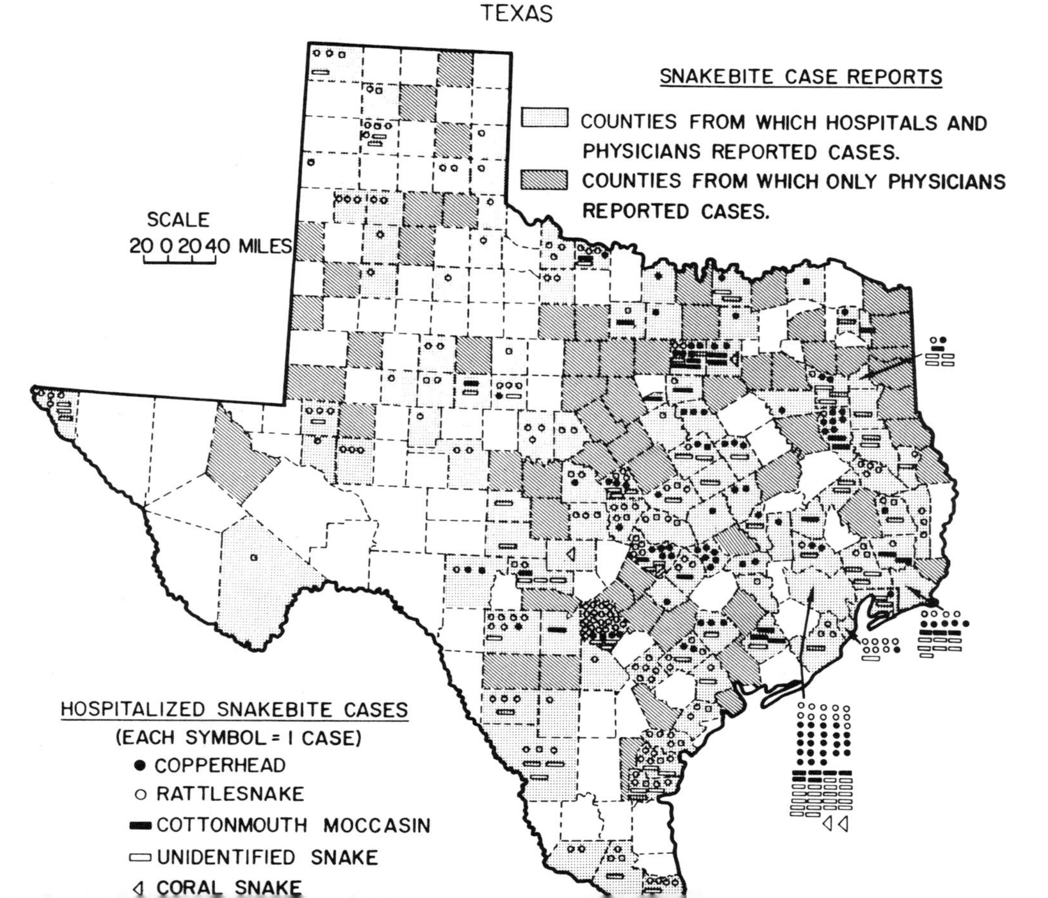
TEXAS
SNAKEBITE CASE REPORTS
COUNTIES FROM WHICH HOSPITALS AND PHYSICIANS REPORTED CASES.
COUNTIES FROM WHICH ONLY PHYSICIANS REPORTED CASES.
SCALE
20 0 20 40 MILES
HOSPITALIZED SNAKEBITE CASES
(EACH SYMBOL = I CASE)
COPPERHEAD
RATTLESNAKE
COTTONMOUTH MOCCASIN
UNIDENTIFIED SNAKE
CORAL SNAKE

CHAPTER I

Prevention of Snakebite

"An ounce of prevention is worth a pound of cure." No better use of this often quoted phrase could be suggested than in the case of animal envenomations. First rule is to *leave them alone!*

The greatest cause of snakebite is the careless handling of poisonous snakes. I would put the percentage of at least ten to fifteen percent of snakebite is due to improper handling. A poisonous snake should never be handled except by experts, and even then I warn you about the death of the nationally known snakebite expert, Dr. Fred Shannon.[1]

A great deal of misinformation is prevalent about a snake wantonly attacking. Of snakes of North America, this can be answered in one short sentence. They will not. If you should happen to walk within the length of any of our poisonous snakes and see it, merely back up or detour to a safe distance. This applies to our formidable seven or eight foot rattlesnakes as well as to the diminutive pigmy rattler or coral snake. They want no trouble. Their greatest desire is to avoid a conflict.

Another thing that should be emphasized is never to pick up the decapitated head of a dangerous snake. I know of a case of the severed head of a moccasin biting fifteen minutes after it had been separated from the body. The trunk, itself, and the organs retain their muscular reaction much longer than a warm-blooded animal. Not long ago a nurse at a local hospital excitedly called my attention to the opened body of a copperhead. Five hours after it had been killed, the snake's heart was beating. It was still beating half an hour later when I left the hospital.

I always open the body of a poisonous snake that has bitten a patient when the snake or its body has accompanied the victim to the hospital. As referred to above, many accidents occur because of the careless handling of a poisonous snake. If it has recently fed, the chances are good that the patient has not been badly poisoned. It has wasted some of its venom upon its food, sometimes almost all of it. Generally, but by no means always, a snake will use about one-third of its supply with each bite. If it is teased enough, angered or hurt, it may use all of its ammunition; after this, of course, it is relatively harmless. About two or three weeks is allowed for it to renew its full supply.

A hundred and forty pound woman was brought to the hospital, pretty badly poisoned. Accompanying her was her eight-year-old nephew. A twenty-two inch copperhead had bitten her on the upper portion of her foot and immediately thereafter had bitten the boy on the calf of his leg. She was so badly poisoned that she was hospitalized for a week, while the youngster suffered very little and was released from the hospital within a few hours, none the worse for his experience. This example I saw and helped treat.

A man, a very foolish but fortunate one in my opinion, was bitten on the thumb by a coral snake. He, it seems, had been told that another bite would counteract the effects of snake poisoning and forced the snake to bite him on the other hand. Then he wrapped the snake around his face and was bitten on the upper lip. He suffered very little, if any, damage, not even enough to keep him from working the next day. I read of this instance in a local paper and communicated with a kinsman of his who declared the story to be true. She, a local amateur herpetologist herself, declared that the man had teased the snake quite a bit with a stick before being bitten the first time, and he either broke the fragile fangs or induced the snake to expend all of its venom before handling it. I accept her theory. Nonetheless, it was a very silly thing to do, and the man was an extremely lucky individual. Indeed, this may be the answer to the East Indian mongoose's seemingly immunization to snake venoms.

Another dangerous practice to avoid is walking along the edge of a shallow stream. If you are lost and must follow such a stream, it is advisable to stay in its center, as this type is the home of the copperhead and the water moccasin. The elevation of the bank allows the snake a better chance of a bite on the face or trunk. A wound in either place is extremely dangerous.

Do not take it for granted that a snake likes high weeds and heavy foliage. The fact is that a newly mowed lawn is quite a "drawing card" to the copperhead and coral snake; mainly, in the early morning or late evening, or after a light summer rain.

If you are a suburbanite, beware of that corner in the yard where you throw your bricks, unused lumber or firewood, and compost. These attract rats and mice and are good hunting grounds for snakes, both non- and poisonous ones.

So much for snakebite prevention; now for insects and arachnids. The black widow spider is by far the most dangerous of these. Its nest is a carelessly constructed labyrinth of cross webs, and they are found almost everywhere. The main precaution is not to stand beneath one and attempt to brush it down with a broom or a brush. The black widow has the dangerous habit of letting loose all holds and dropping straight down. If she lands on your bare shoulders or face, you are in serious trouble. In spring or summer keep a sharp lookout for her nest and egg purses in barns, outhouses, or your summer home after it has been deserted for the winter. Also, do not feel you are a bad housekeeper if she takes a notion to build her web in the upper corner of a room in your city home, for the black widow cares not where she domiciles. A country outhouse or the cornice of a million dollar home is all the same to her.

Never peel the bark from a dead tree with your bare hands; you are liable to peel into the retreat of a scorpion or a centipede, or even, perhaps, a black widow.

If you are camping, search the ground thoroughly before spreading your blankets. In an old house, watch out for the black widow and brown spider. When you must go to an outside toilet, look carefully for these small monsters. The most serious black widow accidents occur there, and the bite of a black widow on the bottom or genitals is a dangerous and painful experience. If at night, be guided by a flashlight, and do not be in such a hurry or so sleepy as to forget your shoes.

Always shake out your shoes or boots in the morning. Scorpions and black widows love to crawl in them at night. Step on a fallen log, not over it, and in hill climbing be cautious where you put your hands.

Then there is a caterpillar that causes a very painful, dangerous, and sometimes fatal wound. It is known by many local names: puss worm, ash worm, asp, etc. The asp, as we know it in the South, is a small yellow bug (one inch long is a large one) that deceitfully hides its dangerous weapons beneath a coat of fine, silky fur. These are spines filled with a potent venom that, unlike the hypodermic needle of the snake and the tarantula and the scorpion, break off into the wound and discharge their venom after being imbedded into the flesh. They live on the lower branches of shrubs and trees, mainly rose bushes, gum elastic, hackberry, and elm trees. Colored differently in their short span of life, they may be white, brown, yellow, or mouse colored. Many other caterpillars are mildy venomous to man, but none can compare with the asp.

The tarantulas, I have purposely come to last. Ugly and fearsome looking, the tarantula has been maligned for many years. At the turn of the century, it was supposed by many to be more deadly than a rattlesnake. If you see a hole in your lawn, not unlike a crayfish hole sans chimney, the chances are that it is a tarantula burrow. The tarantula will bite. So warn your children not to poke their fingers into a hole. If one starts crawling across your hand or bare foot, just hold steady and it will slowly crawl off. This advice will hold good for most spiders and insects. Reach down to grab it or even attempt to brush it off and there is a pretty good chance of a bite. If these insects are around your premises, be careful about running around barefoot at night. Stepped on, most insects and spiders will bite.

To summarize, remember the first rule is to *leave them alone!*

[1] "Dr. Fred Shannon, one of the nation's foremost snakebite authorities and coauthor of a snakebite manual for the armed forces, died early today of a snakebite.

"Dr. Shannon, flown here (Los Angeles) from Safford, Arizona last night, died 45 minutes after he was brought to County General Hospital. He was 44 years old.

"He was bitten by a deadly Mojave rattlesnake on a finger of his left hand Sunday while collecting reptiles in the foothills near Klondyke, Arizona.

"Ten specialists at the hospital fought to save Dr. Shannon. Among them was Dr. Findlay Russell, the other author of the snakebite manual.

"Dr. Russell said that Dr. Shannon had been in a coma most of the night since he was bitten and was being treated with antivenin serum.

"Dr. Shannon had suffered minor bites before, but the Mojave rattler is probably the deadliest of North America snakes, said Dr. Russell."

— Quoted from *The New York Times,*
Wednesday, September 1, 1965

CHAPTER II

Identifying The Dangerous Snakes

When the warm, lazy spring days foretell the coming of summer, the home gardener must be aware that the snake season is upon us. To thousands of newcomers to Houston who enjoy the great outdoors, yet are afraid to go into strange woods for fear of snakes, these facts may quiet a few of those fears. There is more danger of lightning than being bitten by a venomous snake; however it may be well to know the few dangerous snakes by sight. All it takes is a little study. Recognize our four bad snakes and study, if you like, the harmless ones with perfect safety. Several of these are not only harmless, but helpful to man. Many feed on other snakes. Not that the good snakes will seek out the bad, but neither will a coachwhip, racer, or other cannibal snake pass up a coral, a copperhead, young rattler, or moccasin if he is hungry.

It is such a common thing to hear the remark, "A snake's a snake. I don't care if it's poisonous or not. I'll kill it just the same."

It is as logical to say, "A man's a man. Whether he's a criminal or a worthy citizen, I'll treat him as a criminal." Viewed from the eyes of justice, the former remark is far more unfair than the latter. It is impossible for a criminal to be known as such by sight alone. While, on the contrary, any snake can be classified as harmless or dangerous by sight. It takes such a slight amount of study to thus distinguish between the harmless and dangerous families of snakes in our country.

There are only four species of snakes here that can

be classified as dangerous to man. Learn to know these and you are perfectly safe in accepting, as harmless, any other kind. When I use the word "harmless" I do so on a comparative basis. Using as a comparison such animals as the squirrel, rabbit, raccoon, or other small wild animals which are certainly not so greatly feared as the snake, but which, nevertheless, will use their teeth to far greater effect than the harmless snake. Any wild animal will bite if carelessly handled. So will most snakes. But the bite of a squirrel is tenfold more painful than that of a six foot coachwhip. In the woods, there is more hazard in a man's being wantonly attacked by a squirrel, a rabbit, or a coon than there is in his being attacked by a coachwhip, spreading adder, or water snake. In addition, reptiles are not subject to rabies, as far as I know.

WESTERN RATTLESNAKES *(Crotalus atrox)*

The rattlesnake is, of course, the most easily identified of the dangerous snakes. It is the largest of our snakes, with a diamond shaped head quite distinct from its neck. There are many misconceptions regarding this species. For instance, it will not always rattle before striking. On warm, sunny days in winter it awakens and is anything but inanimate. Naturally, if the temperature is low, it is sluggish, but it will strike. All poisonous snakes, except the coral, have vertically eliptical eye pupils. Between the lateral nostrils and the eyes is a nostril-like hole on each side of the head, thus the name "Pit Viper." This is missing on all harmless snakes.

Nature was not thoughtless when she chose this most deadly of all American snakes to carry a mark of identification that not only warns through sight many of her creatures such as the nervous deer, the careful horse, and cautious fox, but a characteristic that also announces danger to the ear of her less favored children — the dull ox, sleepy burro, or heedless 'possum. All will show surprising activity at the first note of that sharp staccato whir of warning.

Is the rattle used as a voluntary warning? I think not; indisputably, it is a warning and, as such, has saved the lives of many creatures, as well as that of the writer. But was this warning sounded because of or in spite of the snake's desire? It is *not* true that *any* snake will shake its tail when startled. Few snakes do. However, I have heard a copperhead stir a cluster of dried leaves to such an extent and in such a manner that the sound could excusably be construed as having been caused by a rattlesnake. I had a king snake that beat a perfect tattoo on the screen of its cage at any unusual disturbance in the house.

That the rattle has a purpose, distinct and aside from acting as a benevolent warning, is granted by most naturalists. But, like its use of the forked tongue, no theory has yet been accepted as to just what that purpose involves. The number of rattles do not necessarily tell its age.

In 1931 the distinguished herpetologist of the University of Michigan, the late Dr. Blanchard, wrote to me in part as follows:

> "I think you hesitate a little more than necessary in discussing the use of the rattle. It is of course not provided as a safeguard to other animals. Evolution has been along strictly selfish lines.
>
> "The rattle may be explained as a means of conserving the venom and the life of the snake. If an enemy can be frightened away the snake saves its venom. The latter is designed for killing prey so quickly that it cannot get too far away. Rattlesnakes have lost the power of rapid locomotion and of constriction. They hunt by waiting. They strike a killing blow, and

when the prey is dead, they engulf it. They will use their venom on an enemy if necessary, but when they do that they cannot get food until more venom is made, and that at a sacrifice of much metabolic energy.

"Other snakes shake their tails when nervous or frightened not in imitation of the rattler, but the rattle is a specialization on this widespread characteristic of vibrating the tail in nervousness.

"A recent explanation of the rattle is that it is an adaptation to save the life of the snake from the trampling herds of bison, and perhaps also of the horses that had their evolution on this continent. Rattlesnakes occur only in America and chiefly in North America, and they are primarily creatures of open country. As such, they have been in competition with the grazing herds."

PIGMY OR GROUND RATTLESNAKE
(Sistrurus miliarius)

The pigmy rattlesnake is a little, slate gray fellow, systematically dotted with black spots along its sides and back. The belly is cream colored and marked with dark, thick lance-shaped lines running from the sides to the middle of its body. These lines meet in the middle but seldom touch. The head usually carries a touch of orange. Its eyes are vertically eliptical, as in all poisonous snakes except the coral. It seldom grows longer than eighteen inches, and is generally found in deep, heavy timber lands, where it coils at the foot of some large tree and patiently awaits the passage of a frog or mouse on which it feeds. This snake likes high, sandy ground but it is not unusual to find one near a stream.

Safely camouflaged in the rotted wood of fallen limbs and trees, this diminutive little serpent is a real danger and one that every visitor to its habitat should beware, especially those fixing camp or gathering firewood. The pigmy rattler is so small and self-effacing in its native woods that it is not at all unusual to read in the paper of a tragic ending to a picnic party caused by some member, usually a child, carelessly or thoughtlessly picking up an armload of brush that contained one of these dangerous serpents. So, if wood needs to be gathered, don't send little Dotty or Lew for it, unless you know you are not in a vicinity where the pigmy rattler abounds.

This snake is very active and strikes on the slightest provocation. Unlike the coral snake, which bites only when touched and usually not even then, the pigmy rattler will generally strike any animated object that approaches it within one-half its length. Its rattles are so minute that they can be seen only after a very close search, and I have never heard one rattle. While its bite is not as dangerous as that of its relatives, the larger rattlers or that of the moccasin, I believe that owing to its diminutive size and aggressiveness, this snake causes nearly as much suffering to mankind as either of the other species. It should be killed on sight!

A young pigmy rattler may be confused with a young spreading adder. In fact, the writer was called to the hospital to aid a young science teacher. She was demonstrating to her class the harmlessness of a spreading adder. She would have been right, as the spreading adder is the most harmless of all snakes and it is impossible to make one bite — if her subject had been a spreading adder. Instead, it was a ground rattler, and she was a very sick as well as embarrassed lady!

To distinguish between the two snakes, just remember that the adder is a slow, sluggish, heavy-bodied individual marked with splotches, and the pigmy rattler is, in comparison, a quick, active, slender serpent marked with decided uniform dots. Then, too, look for the adder's habit of spreading its head and the slight touch of yellow usually appearing on it.

WATER MOCCASIN *(Agkistrodon piscivorus)*

The moccasin is the only poisonous water snake. It can bite under water, much information to the contrary. Although few deaths are an aftermath of its bite, the moccasin causes a very painful wound.

The variation of the color scheme of the moccasin during the different phases of its existence may mislead the investigator. The young one is a brilliant colored little fellow. The ground color is a light brown, sometimes almost gray, patterned with darker splotches. Showing its close relationship to the copperhead, the young moccasin displays a sulphur tipped tail as also marks the young copperhead. This sulphur color disappears as the snake ages and merges into a deep, muddy color. Also, the pattern fades and as an old adult sometimes turns blackish, or extremely dark sans any distinguishable pattern. The lighter hues are almost obliterated, except when observed directly after shedding its old skin.

There is a light, almost yellow stripe along each side of the head which runs horizontally from the neck to the point of the head. This stripe entirely covers each side of the mouth and gives the snake an appearance of having a fixed, satanic grin. *Look for this.* It is the most distinctive mark by which a moccasin can be recognized.

Another feature, easily noticed, is its belly. The moccasin's belly is colored a dull yellow, splotched with black. It is entirely lacking the bright colors found so conspicuously on the majority of harmless snakes. Remember the moccasin has no vivid colors above or below. Do not accept the prevailing theory that any short dark, heavy-bodied or "stump-tailed" snake must necessarily be a dreaded "cotton mouth." Snakes, like human beings, may be fat or slender according to their individual habits. I have seen some rather slender moccasins and also some very fat water snakes. Birth is given alive and the young are about six inches.

When annoyed or startled it flings itself into a coil and opens its mouth. Against its black background, the interior of the gaping mouth appears as white as cotton, giving us another mark of identification and the Southern term "cotton mouth" moccasin.

While the moccasin may occasionally visit clear running streams, which are the hunting grounds of that very interesting and delightful active water snake whose only sin is that of stealing a string of fish that may be dangling in the water at the side of a fisherman, (such a snake is also commonly known by the frightful misnomer "rattlesnake moccasin") its usual habitat is in keeping with its appearance and disposition — a dried creek bed, a small wood pond, or along the edge of a swamp or bayou. The moccasin likes water, but it is not unusual in a dry season to find one several miles away from any lake, pond, or stream seeking a new habitat.

COPPERHEAD *(Agkistrodon contortrix)*

The copperhead is a relatively small, rather sluggish, very dangerous, vicious little rascal. Its very appearance is deceptive. Coiled in a fence corner, among the many hued leaves of an autumn season, this reptile again portrays the brush of nature. Its camouflage is amazing. Many are the harvesters who have had their hands within a few inches of this dreaded little snake, plucked the fruit, and moved on and away from the vicinity, never realizing that an inch more and they would have withdrawn a hand aching with that stinging, burning sensation felt only by one who has been snake bitten. Mind you, the snake knew that the hand was in striking range as it also knew that if it remained perfectly inert, by all odds, it would divert a conflict in which it would probably lose its life. Had the hand moved one inch further—that would have been another thing.

This snake is a ground snake but it is a good climber. It is found everywhere . . . woodlands, prairie, rocky territory, or bordering waterways. Occasionally, during July, August, and September, the copperhead may be found high in a tree. This is when the cicadas (sometimes called locusts) are enjoying their short three month period of their seventeen years of life as a perfect insect above ground. During these months seldom is one of these snakes opened without discovering the remains of a partially digested cicada.

Beautifully colored, the ground color is a pinkish-brown with rhombs of a deeper copper color on its sides connected by a more narrow band of the same color that stretches across the apex of its back. This pattern is like an hour glass. Its belly is of a lighter pink, mottled with occasional very dark copper colored blotches. It is nature's masterpiece of camouflage, but when that fails as a protection it has a weapon that is well deserving of the respect so generally granted it.

While the hospitals report many more snakebite victims due to copperhead bites than those of any other venomous snake, death from their bites has never been reported in or around Houston. However, the effects of its poison is very painful and, of course, death is possible. Individual sensitivity, treatment, position of the bite, amount of venom injected, and side effects of serum should all be taken into consideration. In addition, the age and condition of the patient *and* snake have a bearing. It is well to note here that a snake can voluntarily withhold its venom and also that a snake wastes much venom when teased, and does not have the usual supply immediately after it has eaten. A local harmless snake frequently mistaken for the copperhead is the hognose snake. This mistaken identity may account for the fact that most of the poisonous snakebites reported in the Gulf Coast Region are due to the copperhead.

CORAL SNAKE *(Micrurus fulvius)*

Now we come to the most controversial of our venomous snakes. That they are armed with a venom comparable to that of the cobras and mambas and other deadly elapids is undisputed. But that their bite is sure death, as commonly believed, is nonsense. The writer has seen and personally identified eighteen cases of their bite. No one case was as serious as that of a copperhead. Coral snakes are supposedly rare. Not so!

Several years ago *The Houston Post* newspaper, through Mr. McWhinney, asked that reported sightings of coral snakes be sent to me. One hundred and thirteen reports were made in a three month period, and this is in a radius of twelve miles of the City Hall. There were also forty other reports made that were discounted because of suspected inaccuracy of description. This alone belies the rarity of the coral snake in this vicinity.

Written inquiries throughout the country to doctors, hospitals, and scientists such as Dr. Russell, Dr. Parrish, and the late Dr. Jackson (all men gave or are still giving much study to snakebite) uncovered only five cases of death caused by the coral in the past fifty years. This research covered the entire United States where corals range. Please understand me, the coral is no plaything. Far from it. It should be treated with all the carefulness due any venomous snake.

Even among the best authorities there is question as to its dangerousness. Ditmars, while granting this snake an unusually gentle disposition, warns of its treachery and virulence. Barbour also notes the rareness of reported coral snakebites but assumes that of these few bites, at least 70% were fatal. Hornaday says that a person must make special arrangements with a coral before it can be induced to bite, and Major Scott does not class it with the harmful snakes of America. Colonel Crimmins, colleague of that outstanding student of snake venoms, the late Dr. Dudley Jackson, both of San Antonio, Texas, considers the coral snake the least dangerous of our poisonous snakes. My studies collaborate Crimmins' findings, but when such men as these differ so widely on the subject of the coral's venom, I shall certainly not attempt a judgment. It is sufficient to say that the coral snake is considered a relative of the cobra, is armed with the weapons of a dangerous serpent, and is accused of having used those weapons with fatal results.

Therefore, I shall confine myself to a description of the coral snake and advise the individual who may come upon one of these rare little reptiles to admire its beauty and to study its habits, but not to be friendly with it.

These snakes spend most of their time in burrows and come out on rainy, warm days in the twilight and early morning. As all snakes, they hate glaring sunshine . . . except that they hate it more! All snakes are nocturnal.

The subject seldom exceeds two feet. However, there have been nearly four foot corals reported by authoritative herpetologists. Those generally found will average only eighteen to twenty inches.

Most local snakes marked with rings of red, yellow, and black are coral snakes, but we should not assume that all snakes marked with these colors are venomous. Many, marked with the same colors — but in different order — are harmless. The coral snake's nose is always black. However, there are some "mimics" whose noses are black, although the noses of most of these are red. Yet albinism and melanism, occurring but rarely in all animals, should not be ignored. Beware of a black nose followed by a yellow bonnet, a black band, a yellow ring, and then uniform markings; i.e., yellow rings separating red and black wide bands. These bands and rings encircle the entire body until the tail is reached. Here the red plays out and the yellow rings get wider and alternate with the black bands. The red areas are always marked by occasional black scales (look for these) sometimes so profuse as to almost obliterate the red color completely. I am describing our Texas coral snake *(Micrurus fulvius tenere)* . . . the only coral that ranges in Texas.

There are a few species of harmless snakes that may easily be confused with the coral snake. Most striking are the Arizona king snake, and the Mexican milk snake. These are both marked with identical colors as those of the coral snake, but differently arranged. These king snakes have red and yellow bands separated by a black ring. To distinguish between the dangerous and the harmless, remember the *poisonous* snake has *yellow* rings and red and black wide bands, while the *harmless* ones have *black* rings and red and yellow wide bands, even sometimes white wide bands.

The fangs of the coral snake, unlike those of the other venomous snakes of this territory which are hinged to the maxillary bone, are always erect and very fragile. A twenty inch coral has fangs not much longer than a bumble bee's sting and are easily broken. Therefore, it is difficult for the fangs to penetrate clothing. Someone wrote years ago, and it is still prevalently quoted that these snakes must find a tender, loose fold of skin to poison. This old quote may make sense. I attended a ten year old boy, bitten twice on his shin four inches above his ankle. The youth did everything wrong except kill the snake and bring its body to the doctor. He ran one-half a mile to his home and his father cut across the wound and attempted oral suction; then he used warm packs. Nevertheless, I saw him the next day and he was playing softball. He had vomited twice, but the doctor agreed that fright could have caused that. (Fright has been known to kill.) Otherwise, he showed no symptoms of poisoning. In fact, it is my opinion that the coral is the least dangerous snake in Texas.

To sum up the physiological characteristics of snakes in general and of poisonous snakes in particular, all snakes have pointed teeth fused to the jawbone, a slender tongue, and the two halves of the lower jaw are connected by an elastic ligament.

A hard, transparent covering over the eye protects the cornea, although snakes have no eyelids as such. All poisonous snakes except the coral have vertically eliptical eye pupils.

All "Pit Vipers" have a nostril-like hole between the nose and eyes. This is missing on all harmless snakes. The sense of smell is well developed in all snakes, but the tongue is the snake's most important sensory organ in its reaction to outside stimuli.

No snake has a voice; however, all are capable of hissing. Rattlers have a special sound and some vipers make a swishing noise. Teeth are sometimes broken off, but are replaced by others fastening themselves to the jawbone. Venom is a clear, straw colored liquid released by both fangs and teeth.

The coral is the only poisonous snake to have a head not much larger than its body, which is a characteristic of most harmless snakes.

All but the rattlesnakes have a mottled belly but many harmless snakes are also so marked. There are no venomous snakes that are marked on the dorsal or topside with stripes running from head to tail.

Through evolution limbs, body, and tail parts were fused together to provide a horizontal, lateral, undulating forward movement substituted for locomotion through the dense vegetation of the tropical jungle, where most of the world's 2,000 species of snakes are found.

In most snakes the outer skin is shed in one piece; the snake rubs its body against the ground and struggles to come out head first, turning the skin inside out in the process.

Most snakes lay eggs with a parchment-like shell. Some retain their young until fully developed at birth.

No snake in our country can strike much over one-half its length. Usually, but not necessarily, a snake throws itself into a loop and strikes as far as the loop will extend. They need *not* coil to do this.

Therefore, in closing, a word of caution. Remember, until you identify your snake as harmless, do not go closer than the length of its body. Keep your distance before you become friendly, and stay alive and well.

CHAPTER III

Treatment of Snakebite

Much misery caused by fright or anxiety could be eliminated if snakes were more thoroughly understood. The fact is that approximately 80% of the snakes usually seen during trips to the country are not only harmless, but at least 50% of these are a boon to mankind. Rats, mice, gophers, and many other rodents that cause the farmer untold worry often fall prey to otherwise perfectly harmless snakes. Also there are several species of non-venomous snakes that feed on other snakes. While these cannibal snakes do not seek out the dangerous kind, they do not hesitate to take on a poisonous one, even one that is a larger snake.

In addition, cobra venom *(Cobroxin)* is being used as a non-addictive painkiller for cancer, and rattlesnake venom is used in the treatment of leukemia. Hopefully, research will continue Stimson's experiments in the field of a non-allergic snake serum from rattlesnake venom and kingsnake blood base.

A poisonous snake should never be handled under any circumstances, especially by a novice not familiar with their habits. In all cases of snakebite, the victim should not be alarmed to the slightest degree if the bite is not followed by intense burning pain around the wound, and then local swelling. These symptoms appear within the first five minutes following the bite. Only in the case of a coral snake is there a delayed reaction of pain and swelling, and that not often.

In case of a bite, there are usually two marks made close together from the fangs of the snake. If venom is injected, there will be one of two protein agents present in the released liquid — either "*neurotoxic*" or "*haemolytic.*" The former causes paralysis and general prostration with difficulty in breathing; the latter causes no paralysis, but prostration and local swelling of the affected part, which may in turn become gangrenous due to destruction of tissues. After the bite, assume the snake was poisonous until caught and proved otherwise.

In spite of "backwoods surgery" deaths were rare in the old days, but if medical help is available within an hour's time, there is no excuse for such today. Sterile hospital conditions are mandatory to avoid infection. We have all heard of "old wives" remedies of kerosene, whiskey, gunpowder, rusty razor blades, glass, permanganate of potash, searing of the wound with hot irons, and even as Mary Austin Holly described in her *Texas* in 1831, "use the snake's body as a poultice." Beware of these practices as some are used even today.

Contrary to general belief, snake venom travels very slowly through the system. A substance too irritating to be dissolved by the blood, snake venom backs up into lymphatics and is slowly absorbed by their fluids and then courses through the system, breaking down the tissues and destroying the cells as it goes, causing what is known as "sloughing off" of the flesh. For this reason it is important that the victim lie down and not panic, as excitement or exertion speeds up the process.

There are controversial methods of treatment; however, it is universally agreed that basic steps are as follows:

WHAT TO DO

1) Try not to panic. Lie down.
2) Attend to the victim first; find and kill the snake later.
3) Apply a constricting band loosely 3 inches above the wrist or ankle so that only the lymphatic flow is retarded. Tie another above the elbow or knee. (L-C method

uses tight band.) Release both constrictors every 2 minutes.

4) Cracked ice wrapped in a cloth will help relieve pain and retard spread of poison. (L-C method recommends complete immersion of member in crushed ice in water.)

5) Sip coffee, Coke, or teaspoon of spirits of ammonia. The use of alcohol in snakebite cases is not recommended by *any* authority.

6) If alone, walk slowly toward help; if with companions be carried to car.

7) Get medical help as quickly as possible. Let doctor decide on incision, antivenin, anesthetic, analagesic, or serum.

8) Take the snake with you. It may not be poisonous!

WHAT NOT TO DO

1) Do not get hysterical. (You may die of a heart attack.)

2) DO NOT RUN!

3) Do not attempt self surgery or allow anyone else other than a physician to do so unless bitten by a large rattler (*atrox*) or a moccasin and medical help is more than an hour's drive.

4) Do not use antivenomous serum except in dire emergency as above.

5) Do not drink alcoholic liquor.

6) Do not squeeze wound to stimulate bleeding.

CONTROVERSIAL MEDICAL TREATMENTS

Stimson writes that "for some time I have been quite interested in the arguments that Shannon and Stahnke are having in regard to Stahnke's L-C (Ligature-Cryotherapy) treatment.[1] I have received personal letters from each of them.

"As to the treatment of so-called poisonous insects and probably coral snakes, I think that Dr. Herbert L. Stahnke, Chief of the Bureau of Poisonous Animals of

Arizona, writer of Arizona State College Bulletin, *Treatment of Poisonous Bites and Stings* has come forward with a very interesting, intelligent, and masterly treatise on the treatment of these kinds of accidents, especially the scorpion. Although it is revolutionary in regard to snakebite, he has had great success in the treatment of the only two lethal scorpions in North America. He calls it the L-C Treatment and advises a tight (instead of loose) tourniquet immediately above the bite or sting. [sic — five to ten minutes until tissue temperature can be lowered.] The member is then immersed in crushed ice and water and kept there from 2-7 hours. [sic — 2 hours for sting, 12 hours for smallest snake, 2-6 days for pit viper.]

"While I emphatically disagree with Stahnke regarding his treatment for a venomous snakebite, we seemed to have been quite successful in using his method in the treatment of scorpion, centipede, and tarantula bites, but I have not as yet had an occasion to observe its results upon the victim of a black widow bite."

In his further rebuttal of Dr. Stahnke's L-C treatment, Stimson wrote to Dr. J.W. Albalos, Institute Nacionale de Microbiology, Hospital Independencis, Santago del Estero, Argentina: "I stand for the Jackson theory of continuous suction for as long as 8-20 hours and ice for not over 6-8 hours." To his coauthor, Dr. Englehardt, he wrote that "unless the bite is on the face, neck, or trunk, or the snake is a large moccasin or rattler (*atrox*), put the wounded member in ice, apply a loose constrictor, and let a physician do surgery; i.e., if a doctor is available within an hour's time. I suggest the use of antivenin *only* in the most critical cases."

Dr. Stahnke does not recommend incision or antivenin, but he cautions physicians: "The L-C method does not recommend the injection of any additional fluids around the site of the bite as this causes serious edema and hastens tissue destruction."

Stimson continues with the argument that out of 800 cases he has attended in the past 20 years, there have been no amputations with the I-S (Incision-Suction) method recommended by Dr. Dudly Jackson. In addition he is fearful of prolonged water immersion causing "trench foot," gangrene, and amputations from use of the L-C method. However, Stahnke counters with a recommendation to use a handkerchief as a shield between the ligature and skin to avoid surface damage, and to put the affected part in a plastic bag if it must remain in the iced water over 4 hours. If ice is not available, he suggests a damp compress sprayed with freon or carbon dioxide, and the frozen pad placed on the bite. Stahnke contends, taking these precautions, it has been proved that tissue refrigerated for several weeks does not degenerate into gangrene, thus causing amputation of limb or digit.

No better explanation of how Stahnke's method works than the terse direct quote on page 20 of the bulletin mentioned above, as follows:

> "The chemical action of venom in the body becomes harmful only when the natural defenses of the body are overwhelmed. The ligature holds the venom at the site of the injection until the temperature of that region can be dropped. This lowered temperature causes the tissues to contract and the capillaries and arterioles to constrict initially. Thus, the venom is trapped and enters the body very slowly if the rest of the body is kept uncomfortably warm. In this way, the venom is distributed throughout the body in an extremely dilute condition—too dilute to cause serious effect.
>
> "In addition to this, the bacteria that enter with the venom enter the body proper in such small numbers and weakened condition that the body defenses may readily destroy them."

Stimson and Stahnke agree on the use of the serum. Quoting Stimson:

> "As to the antivenomous serums, I see no reason for their injection if the bite is on an extremity and not caused by a pit viper. Many of the cases I have seen, even though a skin and eye test were given before injecting the serum, have resulted in very bad serum reactions. In fact, in several cases I am quite sure that the cure was much more severe than the disease.
>
> "As an example, a lady was bitten on her ring finger by a copperhead and she was immediately given an antivenomous serum. Within 2 hours her entire body was a mass of red welts. Four hours later she was in convulsions, her tongue so swollen that she could not speak and her eyes swollen shut. She was hospitalized for 2 weeks, went back to the hospital a month later, suffering from a recurrence of the serum reaction. She told me that for 2 years she suffered untold agonies, and at intervals of 3 to 5 months she had been forced to return to the hospital.
>
> "Certainly, if the subject was bitten by a big rattler, I would advise use of an antivenomous serum, irrespective of the risk of that individual's sensitivity to horse blood base serums.
>
> "The most dangerous snake in North America is the big eastern rattlesnake of Florida. It grows to the length of 8 feet, is very heavy, and is armed with fangs up to 2 inches. It carries a supply of venom in proportion to its giant size. In order of deadliness, the western diamondback rattlesnake of Texas, Louisiana, and other southern states is without a doubt a close runner-up to the eastern rattlesnake. I do not have the temerity to advise treatment for these monsters, but there is little doubt in my mind that real heroic treatment is necessary — immediately! Not a minute should be lost for the tourniquet, lancing, suction, and antivenin in large quantities. Corti-

sone and ACTH do not help pit viper bites, but they are of benefit later in treating serum sickness sometimes resulting from antivenin."

In the 1963 March issue of *Missouri Medicine Journal,* "Intravenous Antivenin in Clinical Snake Poisoning," H.M. Parrish writes:

> "Separate the dosage into three parts (amount of serum to be used depending upon the seriousness of the poisoning).
>
> "Use ⅓ I.M., ⅓ I.V., and the balance diluted in a solution of 20 cc antivenin diluted in 500 cc of saline, and administered intravenously, slow drip. Use up to 120 cc antivenin in critical cases."

Now enters the subject of variability: the age and size of the victim, the size of the snake, amount of venom injected, and most of all the victim's sensitivity to venom and serum. So far no one has been able to analyze the extent of individual sensitivity. Observation of the subject's reaction, hour by hour, is the only criterion by which the extent of the illness may be judged. Likewise, it is impossible to ascertain the amount of venom injected. A venomous snake can be rendered relatively harmless by teasing or having just eaten, or lost a fang, so it is up to the doctor to "play it by ear." Every case is different.

Stimson presents another problem. Sometimes it is extremely difficult to diagnose whether it is a black widow spider bite or a coral snake, especially if the animal was not seen or was mistaken for another animal. He reports that while he has never seen a death caused by a black widow, he has seen several cases and the pain of the patient is excruciating. Calcium glutanate in some cases eases the pain, but not in all cases.

The symptoms of the black widow bite are not always

immediately apparent at the site of the wound. If bitten on the foot or leg, there is a hardening of the muscle up through the thigh and into the abdomen. It constricts the abdominal muscles to such an extent that in one case of a child, it was impossible to tell by touch where the ribs ended and the abdomen began. There is delayed pain at the site of the wound for as long as two to three hours, and many patients have been treated for chronic stomach or colon trouble which was in reality caused by the bite of a black widow spider.

Nevertheless, Stimson contends that there is entirely too much hysteria displayed in connection with snakebites, not only by the victim but sometimes by the attending physician. He tells of the following cases:

> "A little girl was bitten on the arm by a harmless racer snake. The teeth of a small snake of this genus rarely grow large enough to penetrate the skin of the exposed portion of a human being, but in this case the child was bitten on the tender skin of the upper portion of her arm. It seemed that she threw her arm over the back of a porch chair and the snake was lying either along the top of the chair or in some shrubbery overhanging it.
>
> "She must have touched the snake and it retaliated. Had she not seen the snake the odds are that she would have assumed that a splinter from the chair or a sharp twig from the bush had scratched her and continued her play. In that event there would not have been the slightest danger, except of infection that is always present in a case of a scratch whether the scratch be caused by a pin, thorn, or the tiny teeth of a small reptile. But, unfortunately, she did see the snake. She was taken to a local hospital; her arm was lanced in several places

and an injection of antitoxin administered.

"The smallest amount of snake venom injected into the blood of a child will cause extreme, agonizing pain and faintness. Generally, also, there is a feeling of nausea, dizziness, and increased pulsation. This little girl had none of these symptoms. That, linked with the fact that her hospital chart showed that the arm had not swelled after a lapse of two hours since she was bitten (swelling and pain are the very first symptoms of any poisonous snakebite). Surely this should have made the physician hesitate before using a knife or injecting such a painful serum in a child.

"Believing as I do, that many like cases have occurred and are still not uncommon in which the same treatment was and is still being used to *cure* the bite of a *harmless* snake, I cannot refrain from citing another case.

"Even a venomous snake may bite and the effects not be dangerous. Witness another case in which an elderly lady, while digging among her flowers, was struck on the palm of her hand by a small snake. This occurred just two days after the experience of the child and in the same city.

"Fortunately, her doctor was not the hysterical type. He thought it was a copperhead, but since the wound was not painful and as there was no local swelling he saw no necessity of heroic measures. To check himself on the type of snake he sent it to me for identification.

"Upon learning that his classification was correct, I frankly admit that I was puzzled. I again examined the snake's head. The fangs were missing! The snake had lost its fangs shortly before striking its victim and had bitten her with the teeth that lie immediately behind the fangs. Of course there is a slight chance for a small amount of venom to have been injected by the teeth; venom may have leaked from the poison glands and saturated the teeth, but an infinitesimally small amount could thus have been transferred to the victim.

"It is quite common to find a serpent which has a fang missing. Seldom has a snake lost both, but this does happen; occasionally, an examination will disclose four fangs in the mouth. All fanged snakes have a reserve supply. It rarely happens that the reserve appears before it is needed, but such occurrences do

CHARACTERISTICS OF SNAKES *

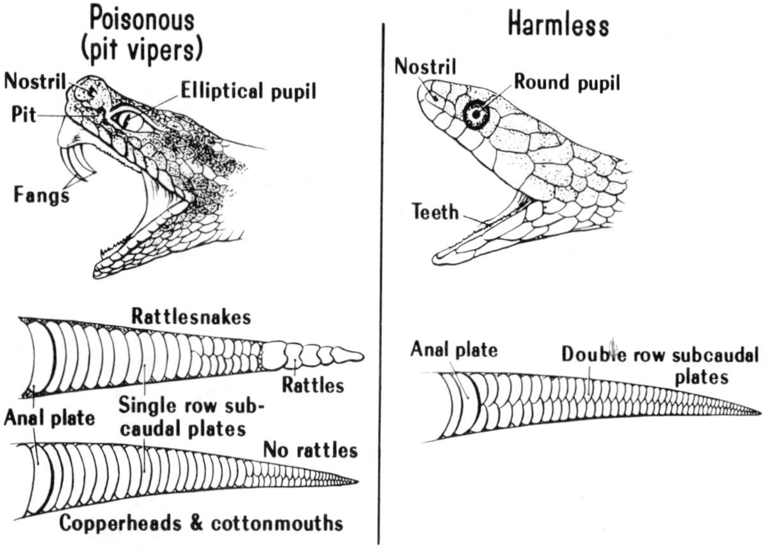

Figure 2. Characteristic Features of Poisonous Snakes (Pit Vipers) and Harmless Snakes.

"Survey of Snakebites in West Virginia," by Henry M. Parrish, M.D., Dr. P.H., reprinted from *The West Virginia Medical Journal,* June, 1964, Vol. 60, No. 6 (pages 143-149).

happen. Normally there is a short lapse between the time that a fang has fallen out or been left in its last victim and the time of emergence of the reserve fang.

"Therefore, I beg all you of the medical profession to 'look before you leap' to conclusions that may not benefit, but actually harm your patient. Know before you 'knife' or 'inject'!" cautions Stimson.

[1] Dr. Stahnke's method of cryotherapy has now been replaced by antivenin as the accepted treatment, according to John E. Werler, Director of the Houston Zoological Gardens.

Figure 11

Figure 12

Reprinted from *Scorpions* by Dr. Herbert L. Stahnke, Ph. D. Published by Poisonous animals Research Laboratory, Arizona State College, Tempe, Arizona. 2nd Edition, 1956, pp. 32-33.

CHAPTER IV

Sizes and Feeding Habits

A great deal of interest is directed toward the feeding habits and sizes of snakes but seldom is this interest stimulated to a degree that compels close study.

After observing a small snake with a head width of a scant half inch engulf an average sized chicken egg, it will be easy to believe the wild and awful tales that deal with the giant snakes of Africa, India, and South America. But we must draw a line somewhere.

Newspapers, always on the alert for a sensational story, are seldom careful to make a satisfactory investigation of facts regarding "tall tales" about snakes. Safe in their knowledge that a libel suit will not be instituted by the subject, newspapers are responsible for the scattering of some amazing stories.

For instance, a reporter on a southern newspaper visiting Brazil gives us one that, in my opinion, tops them all.

In Belem, a small village on the banks of the Amazon, he writes of a gigantic water snake having been killed nearby. "Its head width, *three feet* and its length, *one hundred and twenty-two feet.*" He carries on: "........ there is not sufficient land in cultivation to keep Belem's inhabitants in vegetables. Man, in short, has not conquered the Amazon valley as he did the Hudson and Mississippi ..."

Mark you, I am not quoting Sir John Mandeville or Baron Münchhausen, both of whom saw marvelous sights in the early centuries, but I am quoting from a newspaper in this century.

Of course, any student of herpetology, or for that matter of nature, knows that such a monster would find a horse a tidbit and an elephant merely a good meal. Perhaps we cannot blame the newspapers. Their object is to get circulation and the reading public fairly "eats up" this kind of story. But it is hard on a naturalist to be continuously confronted with: "Why, it must be so! I read it in the newspaper." A simple phone call to any local museum or zoo by the editor would go far toward eliminating these far-fetched yarns.

Doubtless there are larger snakes in the wilds than have been measured, and it is logical to suppose that larger snakes have been seen and have been killed than those that have been exhibited in the zoos of the world or by individual collectors.

There is nothing that can be so overestimated, in my opinion, than a large snake in transit. A calm and conservative observer may well be excused if he "misses his guess" by some few feet. While the maximum length of thirty-one feet is held by some authorities, there is said to be an unstretched anaconda skin in the city of Butantan, Brazil, that measures thirty-three feet. However, in my attempt to get a record of a larger snake than the one now on exhibition in Houston, I received a reply from Dr. Afranio do Amaral of South America and that noted herpetologist made no mention of the skin in Butantan.

Sometime ago a reticulated python of amazing proportions was exhibited in several American cities. It may have reached the thirty-five feet as advertised and it is to my regret that I did not accept the invitation of the owner to make a personal survey.

Later on, a Mr. McClung of Florida, showed three tremendous pythons. The largest, he alleged, was twenty-five feet long and weighed two hundred and ten pounds. All were perfectly gentle. In fact he and his two nieces sat among them and patted their heads.

By his invitation, I entered their cage to examine an inflamed tooth of one of the smaller ones. (I really wanted to make sure of no showman trickery — jaws sewed together, narcotic odor, mouth seared by heat, etc. I found none of these commonly used methods by side-show artists as a protection against their charges. It now seems ridiculous that I should have suspected that anyone would have endangered the lives of so valuable a collection.) The big fellows were as gentle as kittens and one allowed me to extract with my fingers a very loose tooth. It showed no resentment, whatsoever.

It was in 1937 that the Houston Zoological Gardens received Kaa, a reticulated python, native of Sumatra. Kaa had never been sexed (no trifling accomplishment) but, since no eggs were laid, I assume it to be a male. It is and has always been a good feeder.

For reasons not known to me Kaa was not weighed at induction to the zoo. Mr. Tom Baylor, then the head zookeeper and later its superintendent, and Mr. Willis, another zookeeper, join me in the guess that the python was about eighteen feet long and weighed about one hundred and eighty pounds.

In 1953 we weighed and measured him. (The big fellow was very gentle.) He tipped the scale at two hundred and forty-seven pounds after a fast of six weeks. His length was twenty-five feet and a girth of twenty-three inches. I know of no larger living snake and a great deal of correspondence with the greater zoos of the world does not deny my belief.

Although it is a physical possibility that a full-grown man might fall prey to one of these gigantic reptiles, and there is a probability that such has been the case, scientific data notes of no such instance.

The absurdities that deal with large snakes devouring cattle, lions, and other animals of such size belong in such fascinating stories as the Swiss Family Robinson as do the tales of large snakes that lie camouflaged in the foliage of tropical jungles over the native footpaths and swing down their wicked heads to snatch a luckless Indian back into their aboreal habitat and there consume him. But these tales should not be written in natural histories or magazines purporting to be educational.

It is true that occasionally the anaconda, that giant water snake of South America, sometimes awaits its prey from the low hanging limbs of the jungle trees fringing a waterway. Nevertheless, its usual method is to lie in the stream with its entire body submerged, except for the head and patiently wait for the approach of a meal as its victim comes down to drink. Then, lightning-like, its head shoots forward and the prey is pulled into the water and drowned.

Unless the animal is very small there is never a meal devoured in the tree tops. However, the victim usually dies from suffocation; heart and lung action stopped by the strangling constriction of the mighty coils.

The jaws of all snakes are fastened together by elastic-like sinews which allow the back of the jaws to separate and to receive a morsel at least three times the width of the head. This separation is not only present perpendicularly but the jaws are so arranged that they also divide horizontally. The arrangement allows each jaw to advance separately and distinctly from the other three sections, and as one set of teeth are advanced ahead of the others, these in turn are retarded so that the snake seems to advance over its prey instead of pulling the prey inside its throat.

As the meal progresses the snake seems to be in real agony. There are long breathing spells in which the diner merely rests; the head is so distended that it seems to be on the verge of explosion; each scale is separated from its normal position. After the victual is in the throat the game is won, for it quickly passes on to the stomach and then the snake begins the hard task of readjusting the jaws. Judging from appearance, readjusting they need. Grotesquely it attempts a yawn. One side of the mouth obeys, but the other seems obdurate. After several trials the paralyzed appearing jaws answer to command; then there is a series of good healthful gasps and the snake is ready to retire to a nearby refuge to "sleep it off."

Truly, Nature was thoughtful when this creature was endowed with an appetite that might be neglected for as long as eight to ten months. Indeed, there is an authenticated instance, reported by Clifford Pope, of a snake living for two years and seven months without feeding. While a snake can do without food for this length of time, it seldom takes advantage of this fact. A healthy snake usually feeds from two to six times a month.

An oft-quoted myth about a snake's feeding habits is that of its licking the food until the morsel is covered with a slimy secretion which aids it to swallow a larger object than could otherwise be possibly done. If the reader will examine the tongue of a snake, I believe I can get an agreement that before an animal so small as a mouse would thus be coated even a large snake would starve before the food was properly prepared. This legend probably owes its origin to the fact that a snake has been seen at the final moment of disgorgement — an act that has been misinterpreted by the observer. Disgorgement is not an unusual action on the part of a snake during the excitement of capture and the disgorged meal is always "slimy."

The snakes of my acquaintance are epicureans, tempermental and as unpredictable in their appetites as a millionaire dyspeptic or a French gourmet. Slinky, my six-year-old Central American boa constrictor weighing only seventeen pounds, used to take three-quarter pound rabbits, two pound chickens, or a hamster or two, until recently. I received him when he was a baby, only eight inches long, and after a forced feeding of a bit of buttered beefsteak, Slinky ate ravenously. A small mouse, a baby rat, a fledgling, or small hamster — all the same to Slinky.

But now, Slinky wants only one day old baby chicks, seven or eight at a feeding. The rascal is over eight feet long now. In the interim he has taken rabbits, full grown

Norway rats, and two pound chickens.

Which reminds me of the time when I loaned Slinky to a friend, and he put a full grown Norway rat in the snake's cage and left it there during the night. Slinky was about five feet long at the time.

Apparently, the snake was not hungry but the rat was. The vicious disposition of the Norway rat is well known and this individual lived up to his reputation. The next morning my friend found the rat well back in a corner licking his chops, and a full two inches of Slinky's tail was missing—only the vertebra remaining. A bit of surgery, and now Slinky is a blunt-tailed boa constrictor.

Previously, I have outlined in general the feeding habits of snakes. Now let me explain a few details. Unless a snake fears its cage-mate, that animal is perfectly safe if the snake is not hungry. I have the privilege of being in charge of the largest snake in captivity, a reticulated python mentioned previously. Kaa does not know what it is to be afraid; he has never been hurt and is very docile. He allows his keeper all manner of latitude. When I wanted to get his exact girth, Tom Baylor walked into his cage, got the measurements for me with the same calm confidence he would use in measuring the dimensions of a horse. While capable of engulfing a fifty or sixty pound animal, Kaa is content with two or three six pound ducks or rabbits some three or four times a month, or he may refuse food for several months.

Again, I am intrigued by a snake's control of its power and its consideration of wildlife conservation. (Mankind could do well to apply the same principle.) Ordinarily, the big fellow lets us know when he is hungry by raising his posterior about four feet and meandering around his cage. If not hungry, the duck or rabbit that is offered to him is as safe as if in its own pond or hatch. It is amazing to observe the total lack of interest the snake shows in its guest. I have seen a duck waddle back and forth across the folds of the python, apparently unafraid and disinterested in its dreadful cellmate, only looking for an outlet from a strange environment. The rabbits, unconcerned, hop here and there, across, and even upon their host with utter abandonment. Disgustedly, Kaa will move this way or that in attempts to be rid of the pests, but never a show of anger.

This is Kaa when he is not hungry.

When he is, he seldom fools around about it. There is a lightning-like flash of his huge head, a squeal or a quack and — dinner is served! Let us get one thing straight. That duck or rabbit dies quickly. The snake reaches out instantly, enfolds its prey in a deadly embrace, stopping its heart action by suffocation. (Prey of a poisonous snake suffers an almost instantaneous death. True, the prey of a racer, garter snake, hognosed snake, or a whip snake has no easy time of it.) But I hold that unless he is a vegetarian, man with his slaughter-houses, his fishing, and hunting expeditions should go slow before condemning the snake for its mode of survival.

It is generally supposed that a snake will take only living food. That is not a fact. Freshly killed animals are often preferred by some snakes. However, this food must be served before rigor mortis has set in; seldom will a snake take dead food unless it is warmed to body heat.

Live food is a subject I bring up — because of a criticism to which I was recently subjected. My prosecutor was an outstanding sportsman. He was indignant when I answered his inquiry that we feed live animals to the reptiles at the zoo. He was not only indignant; he was horrified and shocked! This from a man who thinks nothing of shooting over a pond filled with wild ducks, killing one or two and wounding perhaps ten of the flock. Also on a safari, wounding an elk, a deer, or a moose and leaving the poor animals to a slow, lingering death; or even killing twenty or more gorillas to capture a baby — this man thinks we, of the zoo, are merciless!

CHAPTER V

Charming

Numerous are the stories of the weird power of snakes in regard to their charming ability. That a snake is endowed with the awesome power to reduce small creatures, such as frogs, rats, and birds to a state of bodily paralysis is commonly granted, but that fact loses most of its interest when it is learned that this happening is caused by the weakness of the victim rather than an uncanny occult power of the serpent.

On several occasions I have heard the shrill, pitiful cry of a frog so different from its normal croak — and found the announcer sprawled on its belly in a decidedly subjected manner, motionlessly waiting the approach of the stealthily advancing snake. In every instance there was ample time for a quick hop to safety; instead, the frog's seemingly paralyzed condition demanded that it remain inert until actually touched by the snake. Whereupon, it again regained control of its being, and the snake found anything but an inanimate victim with which to deal. Occasionally the snake will miss its aim, and merely touch the frog. Then the spell seems broken. For the slight impact recalls to use the normal action of the frog's faculties and it generally makes good its escape.

Copying others' experiments I have slipped behind frogs and with a quiet, undulating motion advanced a long, pliant switch toward them. Several times the resultant cries and actions were the same as if the switch had been a snake. Likewise the actual contact of the switch with the body of the frog again sets in motion its actions, and ceasing to be motionless, the frog hurls itself into a series of frantic hops and soon disappears in the grass. True, only a slight percentage of the experiments developed as above outlined, but the fact that even a few frogs can be fooled into a state of paralyzed fear by a switch properly manipulated, assures me that no snake has any occult powers whatsoever. Although the tiger has never been heralded as possessing supernatural gifts, it has been known to instill in man, himself, such fears as to cause the victim the loss of all bodily movement.

Not satisfied with allowing the snake a mere hypnotic power that reduces its subjects to a state of physical inertia, many of our overzealous nature students go even further and write (as educational papers) articles that allow the serpent the awful power of actually forcing a mentally alert but unwilling victim to approach into the fearful embrace! They allege that the eyes of the snake are so endowed that a small bird or animal permitting its gaze to meet the baleful stare of the serpent immediately finds itself so horribly bewitched that, with pitiful cries and faltering steps, it tremblingly obeys the awful edict and advances to its fate.

Recently a close study of the feeding habits of a family of young boa constrictors which I am raising has confirmed some of my earlier opinions. These snakes have had a steady diet of rats and mice with an occasional rabbit dessert. The rabbits were young and were entirely too young to show fear or any other emotion, but full-grown mice and half-grown rats show no fear whatsoever of the snakes. In fact, if put into the snakes' cages, they show only a bit of hesitation in approaching the snake while meandering back and forth in attempts to find a way out of this strange environment.

If the snake is hungry there is a quick strike, a squeak, and dinner is served. However, if the snake is not hungry, and this occurs quite often, it allows the rodent no end of liberties. I have seen a half-grown rat trample across the head of one of my charges and then turn and deliberately nibble at a loose fragment of dead skin that dangled from the snake's lower jaw. The snake showed no resentment, but merely pulled its head back and away from the little nuisance.

I am fully aware that a captive creature is a poor criterion by which to judge their natural behavior and it well may be cited that in their natural habitat, both creatures would have behaved differently. With this in mind, I have placed my young boas in the crotch of a small tree only a few feet from the ground, and then put a full-grown mouse or a half-grown rat on the outer edge of the branch. Many times the rodent was not more than three or four feet above the ground and could have escaped by dropping to the ground. Not one has done this. Clinging to the swaying limb, it studies the situation for a moment, and when its balance is fully achieved it usually will deliberately, unhurriedly, and with no outward show of trepidation, calmly climb higher and often directly on and over the snake! If hungry, the snake sluggishly advances, but on the whole shows very little interest in its meal. If not hungry, it ignores its prey.

Thus, we have another contradiction in the behavior of animals. We have the frog with fears so abject that it becomes paralyzed at the mere suggestion of an approach through the grass of a snake—or a switch. On the other hand, we have creatures, the natural food of most snakes, creatures of much higher origin, creatures more intelligent, creatures that have been fabled in the history of mankind for their shrewdness ever since man has shown interest in animal behavior — we have these intelligent little beasts showing no fear of a reptile who feeds chiefly on its kind. Why? Certainly charming is not the answer, although charming has its advocates even now, as it did in the day of Aristotle.

While willing to grant that fear will cause a total loss of physical energy, shall we allow ourselves to be led to believe that any normal creature, its senses functioning, will knowingly approach such a fearful death? Is it not against the law of self-preservation? That the senses of all the supposed victims are alert is shown by the fact that one of the high points of the fanciful narrative always intensifies the crying and fearful manner which marks the behavior of the "charmed" creature.

I repeat such ideas are nonsense. They are probably founded on the fact that a snake has been observed in the act of actually capturing a parent bird, which had been too courageous in defending its brood of nestlings. The proximity of a snake in the vicinity of a nest always causes a deep furor, especially if the setting is near the nest of a blue jay. The jay, himself an ogre of the deepest hue in regard to the devastation of a neighbor's nest, is quick to decry the ravagement of its own and full of vim and energy in protecting it. Witness an adventure of mine to demonstrate.

While loitering through a heavily wooded section of South Texas one spring morning, my attention was attracted by the sharp, angry call of a blue jay. I directed my course toward a huge live oak tree, from where the disturbance originated.

There I saw a chicken snake devouring one of a brood of young jays. Upon my arrival beneath the tree I noted that I was not the only curious one, for there had already arrived six jays and several other birds.

The other birds were satisfied to remain merely horrified spectators, or at the most to voice their sympathy to their bereaved neighbors in excited chirps. Not so, however, were the visiting jays. With harsh, ringing calls they launched themselves into the fray with gusto. Indeed, these doughty little reinforcements were so insistent with their cries and actual aerial attacks upon the snake, that it was impossible for me to distinguish between the parent birds and their courageous allies. With a bedlam-like racket the indomitable defenders hovered a foot or less above the intruder until an opening was seen; then, with quick, vigorous darts, they dived-bombed him. More than once I saw them make direct contact and have good reason to wonder that the reptile could have withstood the onslaught.

It did, however, after devouring all but one of the small birds. Then the snake hurriedly meandered its way along a large limb of the oak tree into a smaller tree and disappeared in the foliage of a trumpet vine.

The screaming mob of angry jays, now double the initial flock, flew so close to the departing marauder that I marveled not only at their intrepidity, but also that the snake made little attempt to defend itself.

Rarely will a bird, unable to fly, leave the nest even in the face of such a direful situation. However, exceptions do occur. During the first few minutes of the invasion one of the fledglings either jumped or was ejected from the nest and now that the fight had ended, I presumed to take a small part in the fray. I picked up the little fellow and was attempting to aid it in adjusting its balance on a lower limb of the tree when, with startling speed, the parent bird launched down and struck me a ringing blow above the eye. The wound was deep enough to bleed freely, and as I stanched the flow I felt badly that my motive should have been so grossly misconstrued.

From this experience I can easily imagine a casual observer, noting the assemblage of the jays attracted toward the snake, allowing himself to fancy that the attraction was due to conjuration, especially if he were of the class of students who allow their wishes to guide conjectures. Eagerness to discover the supernatural in the lives of wild creatures often tempts us to disregard the ordinary, however evident, and substitute the mystic.

CHAPTER VI

Is The Spreading Adder a Remarkable Actor?

The spreading adder does not exhume a deadly fume with its breath nor does any other serpent.

In regard to this much maligned creature, it should be recited that contrary to its supposed deadliness, it is really the most harmless of the so-called harmless snakes of our country. The chicken snake will collect a few eggs as just toll for ridding a barnyard of rats and mice. To satisfy its overwhelming curiosity, the coachwhip will actually chase a fleeing mortal. The king snake will occasionally be found as an unwelcome guest in the house.

All three of these so commonly granted harmless snakes will bite with their tiny teeth if treated too familiarly. But the spreading adder's only vice is a strong desire to impress the trespasser with an entirely assumed aspect of furiousness. It seeks a habitat as far from the domicile of man as it can find.

Suppose that we suddenly walk within a foot or two of this preposterous "bluffer." What is the result? We see a horrid coil of about three feet of as ugly and fearful a serpent as can be imagined. Comparable, in appearance, with the terrible gaboon viper of Africa, the "fer de lance" of South America, or the deadly king cobra of India, our first desire is to kill such a monster, but suppose we refrain a moment or two to make an observation.

We take a stick and prod it gently. Immediately, we are startled, as with a loud blowing hiss, the ungainly spring uncoils and lashes out at the implement. But, notice closely now, and we shall see that it strikes with its mouth closed!

Repeated efforts fail to excite it to a more drastic action, so we change our tactics. Exchanging our stick for a more pliant limb, we gently switch the back of our subject. There is also a noteworthy change in its defense. It uncoils and attempts, in its characteristic sluggish manner, to escape the tormentor.

We, using our switch as a rein, turn it from this root, from that hole, and cut off its attempted retreat into a nearby clump of bushes, and then a surprising thing transpires. The snake's efforts to escape have gradually been relaxing; its frantic aggressive counterattacks that marked the beginning of the experiment have lulled into a tired, listless writhing as it seeks now only to escape the tantalizing of the switch, which is used only to bar its way to refuge and in no way as a lash.

Now it collapses. It is on its back. A slimy saliva is dripping from its mouth, followed by the hind legs of a partially digested toad. Excrement is also emitted. Its tongue, that carefully guarded organ of sound transmission, is protruding from its mouth and lolling in the dust. Careful examination does not disclose a sign of breathing.

Have we killed it? Were it not for the fact that the twisting and writhing of the tail, so prevalent in all dying reptiles, are absent here, we would certainly affirm that we had. But we stoop and turn the snake over on its stomach, and are amazed to see a quick contraction of muscles, and the snake has again assumed the position of a logically dead snake, stomach skyward! Repeated efforts failing to change the situation, we assume a quiet, waiting attitude, and watch for developments.

Within a few minutes, the tongue is withdrawn and our victim slowly turns again in the position of a live snake, and as we watch it slowly wend its way toward a clump of bushes we still find ourselves wondering if the snake was really frightened into a state of anesthesia or did it feign death as nature's protective device.

Here again is an unsettled question among those who have given their lives to the study of reptiles, but I shall venture to set forth a rather extensive experiment to which one of these snakes was recently subjected.

I have experimented quite a bit with the hog-nosed snake in an attempt to learn the cause of these convulsions which terminate into seeming lifelessness. The most important fact that I have noticed is that this unusual trait is called upon only once — at the time of capture. Although the snake may have several seizures at the time of capture, it never attempts the same behavior as a captive. This, at least, has been the behavior of a number of snakes that I have observed. Only one has ever been induced to play the game a second time. Not all of the adders that I have tested for this mannerism have reacted exactly the same.

In fact, only about 50% would feign death, no matter how treated. Those that did, usually tried to escape first, then "bluffed," and, seemingly, as a last resource threw themselves into a series of contortions which ended in feigning death.

Occasionally, however, I have found those that feign death the instant they were touched. The fact that all of these snakes disgorged immediately before going into the convulsion preceding the faint has led me to believe that it was a natural loss of consciousness caused by fear, instead of a conscious trick. Nevertheless, a recent experiment proved, to me at least, the fallacy of this thought. I will admit that I could see no argument against Ditmar's theory that an unconscious snake will not continuously revert itself to an unnatural position when placed in a natural one, but their actions otherwise were such that I could not but believe that the convulsions were bona fide.

Recently, I found an adder that at the first touch threw open its mouth and disgorged a portion of a toad and immediately turned over on its back. I allowed it to stay in that position while I kneeled down near it, but out of vision. Its mouth was wide open and its tongue was lolling out to one side. The first sign of life was the withdrawal of the tongue and a nearly imperceptible closing of the mouth. I slightly touched its upturned stomach, whereupon, flinging wide its jaws and with protruding tongue, the snake again took the normal position of a dead snake.

A small pool was nearby and I conceived a more drastic test. It was not a water snake with which I was dealing and I knew that although all snakes are good swimmers, not even a water snake can lie on its back, its mouth open and tongue out, for the same length of time under water that this suspected trickster was now doing. Already ten minutes had passed and the snake was still inert. Surely, if it is "possuming" it will not carry the matter to such an extent that it will drown rather than be exposed! Then again, that little trick of reverting its body. Will it still insist upon turning itself upside down if suddenly submerged in a bath? If the coma is not a trick what will be the result? If the snake is in a state of unconsciousness, as held by many students of biology, it will lie on its back until it drowns. It is incapable of conscious movement. If, on the other hand, it is feigning, as I suppose, there will be a quick dash for shore.

Naturally gifted, or cursed, with a timid disposition in regard to causing pain or suffering to my fellow creatures in an attempt to satisfy an abnormal curiosity as to their habits and modes of life, it is with a sincere wish in my mind that I shall prove this serpent to be a remarkable actor and not a chronic epileptic that I proceeded to follow up my experiment.

With watch in hand, I gently submerged the subject belly down into the pool. My anticipation of a quick dash for terra firma was ill founded. Contrarily, the reverse transpired. For the snake neither closed its mouth nor retracted its tongue, but slowly sank to the bottom with gaping jaws and lifeless tongue. There was a sudden contraction of muscles and behold! It was on its back. It lay thus at the bottom, exactly as it did on dry land. But wait! The tongue was withdrawn and the mouth closed. I glanced at my watch. Fifteen seconds against two minutes on land! That was something. I stroked the upturned stomach. There was a feeble attempt to react the same as portrayed under normal conditions. The mouth opened just a bit and was quickly closed. No amount of "tickling" would change the situation. Now the tongue was darting in and out, the normal reaction of a snake in a strange environment. Then the head gradually seemed to float up and as it broke the surface of the water, the body turned over to the natural position. My watch advised me that fifty-eight seconds, less than a minute, had elapsed since the beginning of the bath.

The adder swam to shore where, upon the first touch, it again fell into a pseudo faint. Oh, no, you preposterous bluffer, you cannot fool me again, not with the same bag of tricks! Back to your bath.

This time the snake did not even attempt to turn over. Contact with the water recalled past experience and it immediately swam ashore and acknowledged fraud. For now no manner of handling would result in a faint or feigning death. So, feeling that this particular fellow had divulged to me a secret, though grudgingly done, I saw no reason why it should not spend the rest of its days in the peace and quiet of the broad prairies that were its home, and as it glided into a crayfish hole, I could only wish it well and hope that I had not instilled into it a sense of false security in its dealings with my kind.

As I drove home my feeling of perfect satisfaction as to having settled a debatable question of the reptile world was grossly shattered by a thought that it was very possible that the snake may have been unconscious and the cool water had merely revived it.

I wonder!

(Reprinted with permission from *Field and Stream Magazine*)

CHAPTER VII
The Milk Snake

Here we have fact and fancy very closely interwoven. Yes, there is really a milk snake. It is a small harmless snake that chooses mice and rats as its usual diet; therefore, is attracted to the stables and milk houses of rural farms and dairies by the hordes of these rodents that live in and around that vicinity. But you need not be too careful in your classification of the milk snake when visiting the country. If you visit an area where the black snake is common you will be told that it is a "milk snake," or if the chicken snake is the most common, it will be called a "milk snake." Indeed, I have even heard the term used whereby an indigo snake was so slandered. For years I was puzzled by this much talked-of snake. I have traveled many miles to quiz a farmer friend who had killed a milk snake, only to be shown the remains of a chicken snake. On other occasions I have had pointed out to me an ordinary king snake or the blue racer as representative of this mysterious family of serpents, which hold such sway in the minds of many nature romancers.

At last I gave it up as a bad job. Be that as it may, I was unable to understand why it was that nearly everyone whom I consulted (mostly dairymen and farmers about the milk snake) had seen one while I labored in vain to find so common a creature. I have since concluded that most any snake that is drawn by the natural desire to visit a community thriving with rodents that form its usual diet must gain for itself the title of "milk snake." This title applied merely because it was seen in the barnyard and because it was a snake. The hasty conclusion was formed that its visit was not strictly honorable. Concluding that the cows were the attraction and being unable to otherwise connect the snake and the cow, many individuals assume that the cow is misappropriating her milk in favor of the snake.

Weird and fanciful tales are thus founded. They range from the romantic narrative, in which a sedate old bossy with an otherwise irreproachable reputation has not only willingly but gladly responded to the wiles of a serpent and actually has been observed, night after night, eagerly wending her wayward path to a sequestered rendezvous and there allowed the reptile to satisfy its unnatural thirst to a sordid story of a huge cobra wrapping its coils around the legs of a frantic victim and forcing her to surrender her milk.

I do not exaggerate. This cobra story was most graphically portrayed in a sporting magazine under the name of a fellow member of the National Geographic Society.

A noted authority in writing of this alleged peculiarity of the milk snake mentions the incredulity of the statement of a dairyman, that upon noticing the shortage of the usual milk supply of a certain cow, he (the dairyman) substantiated his suspicion by closely watching the animal and at last found her in the act of allowing a snake the privilege generally extended only to her calf. Dr. Ditmars points out the fallacy of this yarn by stating that even granting a snake and cow so unusual alliance, it would be impossible for the stomach of a very large snake to contain enough milk to make the loss noticeable.

After many experiments with individual members of several species of serpents, I found that not one would satisfy its thirst with milk, even though the subject was nearly dead for want of a drink. Moccasins, king snakes, chicken snakes, blue racers, and coachwhips all refused the milk. When a water snake reacted in the following manner to my attempts to inveigle it to take even a swallow of milk, I feel that I can safely affirm that a milk-drinking snake is a fabulous, imaginary creature.

While on a fishing trip along the edge of Trinity Bay, I captured a small snake. Within three minutes I caught a small frog. Not anticipating the act in its actuality, but merely testing a fancy, I offered it to the snake and was surprised to see the offer accepted, not in the manner of an angry striking reptile, but with the more delicate motion of a feeding snake. I then placed the snake in a cage and within the next hour it had engulfed six additional frogs, which were all that were offered.

Surprised by its unusual voracity — most snakes must be kept several weeks before they will eat — I took the little fellow home with me so that I might study this unusual behavior.

Since this snake was such a good feeder, I felt quite sure that it would be an unusually good subject upon which to experiment in regard to milk drinking.

I placed it in a small meshed wire cage and for the course of ten days and nights kept it well supplied with water. Its remarkably gentle disposition allowed it to drink while I looked on, thus signifying that the strange environment did not retard its natural drinking habits. Allowing it a full ten days in which to familiarize itself with its surroundings I removed the water dish and denied it any fluid for the next forty-eight hours. I then filled the vessel with fresh milk and put it into the cage.

Eagerly darting to its accustomed well the little reptile halted within a few inches of the rim and seemed to test the fluid with its tongue. With its head poised over the milk, it hesitated at the side of the glass for ten minutes and then slowly crawled back to the corner of the cage, coiling itself into a resting position. I found it in its usual corner the following morning, the milk untouched. Being offered water, the snake immediately attempted to satisfy its thirst, but this I would not allow until I had fully demonstrated, at least to my own satisfaction, that it would die of thirst rather than to accept the milk as a substitute for water. I kept it well supplied with milk for the following five days and allowed it no water, but it reacted exactly as had my other subjects of my studies. It positively refused to assuage a seven-day thirst with a fluid that many nature romancers assert causes the snake to commit robbery, mayhem, and even murder to obtain.

The result of this experiment convinces me that the drinking of milk by a snake is very improbable and that the nursing of a cow by a species of reptile is a fable that only adds more weight to the already overburdened load of myths under which the serpents labor. Even though you may consider the reptiles as deserving of such stories — think of the cow's reputation. Surely she deserves some consideration.

CHAPTER VIII

The Hoop Snake

Often told is the tale of the hoop snake. Until recently I have never met a person who would still protest after having his story challenged that he had actually witnessed the fearful sight of a snake taking its tail in its mouth and rolling itself, hoop-like and with tremendous speed, toward a prospective victim.

The story is sometimes told in the first person. Usually, however, it is a story that has passed down through generations and the actual originator of the yarn has long since died. However, exceptions do occur.

Not long ago, I was a guest at an informal party and was told the following absurd story by a South Carolinian as an actual happening in which he, himself, played no small part. He was an excellent storyteller and held his listeners to the keenest pitch throughout his recital.

> "The year after I married, my wife's father gave us a small plantation lying several miles north of Beaufort, Louisiana. We moved and lived out there for several years.
>
> "Starting my first spring planting early, I ordered one of the negro tenants to 'plow-up' a certain tract about a mile east of the house. I had noticed that, notwithstanding this fifty acres seemed to be especially good soil for grain, it had not been under cultivation for several years.
>
> "Old Tobe's emphatic refusal to 'pester erroun dat part o' de farm' was explained by

what I supposed at the time to be a foolish superstitious fear of a colony of hoop snakes which, he declared, were always uncovered whenever this particular field was broken. Not once but on several occasions had these serpents been 'plowed-up,' which disturbance so violently riled them that Providence alone was given credit for no fatal results.

"Now, I had always been led to believe that the hoop snake was only an imaginary creature and thought that it would be great fun to impress upon my tenants a degree of courage that I do not possess. I told Tobe that I'd do it myself.

"For the first two days everything went along fine and I had actually begun to experience a sense of disappointment that no snakes had turned up. But the morning of the third, things happened.

"I was sitting on the plow-seat, day dreaming. Snakes were a thousand miles from my mind when those two old plow mules took out. Abruptly tossed from the seat of the plow, I picked myself up and saw a glistening, black snake unfurl itself from a hoop-like coil and launch out at the frantic team of mules.

"Whether or not it struck with its tail, as is generally alleged, I don't know. But I do know that the mule dropped as if shot. It did not even kick or struggle. I did not take time to investigate the death of the second mule — which was found dead beside its mate when we had courage enough to approach the vicinity. At the time my only thought was of escape. I ran toward the house and did not feel safe until I had covered at least a half-mile.

> "No, siree, they can all say 'Thar ain't no sich animal,' but I know better."

Well, what are you going to say about a story like that? Courtesy forbids a challenge, and common sense allied with the teachings of natural science and physiology cry aloud for argument.

I have cited this story not as an example of a terse version of the ordinary "hoop snake yarn," but because it was repeated to me as an actual happening which had been witnessed by the narrator. Such examples are rare.

The usual tale concludes with the fact that the snake's mad rampage always ends as its intended victim jumps behind a tree at the very moment the snake decided to administer the "coup de grace" and the awful blow is delivered to the tree trunk instead. As the venom saturates the tree, it shudders, droops it branches, the leaves tumble and fall upon the head of the bewildered spectator.

Bear in mind, however, that no narrator of this fearful tale has ever troubled himself to the extent that he has captured this monster — dead or alive — and offered it to the scientific world as proof of so mooted a question.

It has long been accepted by science that there is no snake that uses a sting or the point of its tail as a weapon with which to inject its poison. There is, however, a degenerate member of the water snake species that bears a small, horn-like appendage on its tail which is sharp enough to pierce the flesh. The abrasion is seldom deep enough to draw blood and should not be considered in the same light with a sting, a bite, or any other poisonous wound. It is the mud snake.

The broken tail of a "glass snake" when it grows perpendicular to the body is not an unusual occurrence, and this could give to a careless observer a wonderful nucleus around which to weave a highly imaginative narrative about a snake with a "stinger" on its tail!

CHAPTER IX

The Sea Serpent

From the time of Noah to the present, sailors have vied with each other in elaborating the tales of their travels. The stories told by seafaring men of the pre-Columbian period are graphic in their description, and very few of the narrators failed to use the sea serpent to good advantage. The hardy Norsemen embodied a huge serpent in their religion and surpass all other legends in regard to size by allowing their Midgard serpent to encircle the world. Thor battled the serpent, killed it, and in turn was suffocated by the venom which the dying monster vomited over him. It is noteworthy that most religions deal not a little with serpents and as the Norsemen were a nation of sailors, it is not surprising that they chose a snake from the sea to personify a deity.

Just as the Phoenicians and the Egyptians used serpents as figureheads on their ships as exponents of their religions, so did the early Greeks and Romans. What better example than the serpent in the Garden of Eden in the Hebrew religion, on which our own Christian faith is based?

From the earliest Egyptian galleys to the nineteenth century schooners, the voyage was long even for short distances. Verification was nil due to lack of communication. So why should lonesome men of the sea not see animals of the sea, as they stood their respective watches? Common sense, especially tempered by a ration of rum and loneliness, can easily give way to imagination and cause one to visualize in some foreign tropical vine or a peculiarly shaped mass of seaweed a monstrous serpent.

It is not unusual to see newspaper accounts, well authenticated by sworn statements of the crew and passengers of the sighting of a sea monster that, to all appearances, was a huge serpent. Investigation generally discloses a very prosaic explanation, which explanation, because of its casualness, is seldom published and the public is left with the first impression. Pictures of the Loch Ness Sea Serpent of Scotland have even been published!

While granting the possibility that the vast, illimitable depths of the five oceans may contain a super giant snake, all natural scientists agree that the longest sea serpent yet brought before them has never equaled in size that of our largest Florida rattlers.

This snake is a true sea serpent and a dangerous one. The Florida rattlesnake is a real menace not only in our country, but in the South Pacific and all along the shores of the Indian Ocean. There the fishermen of these waters fear them greatly, not so much because of their great size but because of their powerful venom.

Until the middle of this century, most writers of natural history paid very little attention to reptile life. They carefully checked authorities on beast and fowl, but set in writing almost any story they were told in regard to snakes. Thus many monstrosities in the form of educational writing profusely appeared in the eighteenth, nineteenth, and the early part of the twentieth centuries. It is not unusual to find a book written by an eminent scholar, such as Goldsmith, in which versions of sailors' yarns are recited to prove the existence of a gigantic sea serpent. These forgotten stories are recalled only by the mistaken zeal of the editor of a newspaper and used as authority by a nature faker whose story has been too severely criticized.

Then we have the Manderville type of downright liars. In his travels he saw many serpents of "stupendous length and girth," but he also saw two-headed men, and trees that bore meat sandwiches. The gullibility of his generation allowed his stories to be believed in their entirety. But now, while scoffing at the yarns of two-headed men and sandwich trees, there are many of us who are not too incredulous as to the sea serpents he is alleged to have seen.

In the fall of 1932 the coastal population of Spain was thrown into a turmoil by the reported sighting of a gigantic sea serpent. The reports were from several ships and considered important enough to sustain investigation. Exhaustive search was instituted which divulged that a large tree was the cause of the excitement.

During ancient times almost every seaman who ventured a few hundred miles from shore reported seeing sea serpents. If these monsters were really seen, is it not reasonable to expect that during the twentieth century, with ocean liners crowding the traffic lanes and exploration expeditions equipped with high power guns and cameras, that one of these gigantic snakes would have been killed or captured?

Apparently, we must classify as "unsolved problems" the sea serpents along with UFO sightings, "Big Foot," and the Bermuda Triangle — all modern-day puzzles that cannot be solved until all jigsaw pieces are in place. Perhaps a satellite in the space program holds the future answer in its computer. Until then, the scientific world has indexed the sea serpent as a legendary creature, and before that classification can be changed the authorities demand the "corpus delicti." "Venomous animals are found in every state of the continental United States. These include venomous snakes, lizards (Gila monster), toads, spiders, scorpions, centipedes, millipedes, caterpillars, and Hymenoptera insects (bees, wasps, yellow jackets, hornets, and ants). "Among venomous marine animals are jellyfish, stingrays, sculpins, hydroids, sponges, segmented worms, echinoderms, mollusks, and venomous fish (Esse, Halstead, Russell)."[1]

[1] Parrish, Henry M. "Analysis of 460 Fatalities from Venomous Animals in the United States," *The American Journal of the Medical Sciences,* vol. 245, number 2, February 1963.

CHAPTER X

The Coachwhip

Why are snakes generally so badly misunderstood, maligned, exaggerated, and sometimes just ordinarily lied about? How often have I heard a man, whose veracity on all other matters is absolutely above reproach, narrate a hair-raising experience of a coachwhip whipping a man, and if challenged on the truth of his story will positively substantiate it by downright declaring that he saw it!

It is true that a coachwhip will, on rare occasions, follow an unaccustomed sight. For instance, I was followed for probably a quarter of a mile by an unusually large snake of this species. This happened in a small prairie that was surrounded for a radius of about a mile with a semi-tropical thicket. I noticed the snake just as I left the foliage. With his head (which angled about 90 degrees from his neck) reared about two feet from the ground, he was calmly watching my every motion. When our respective curiosity was satisfied, or rather mine was satisfied, I continued my tramp.

After a few hundred feet I paused for some trivial reason and was surprised to see another (as I then thought) snake in the same identical posture as the other one which I had just left. While it is nothing very uncommon to run across a coachwhip on a Texas prairie, I had never before seen two large ones in as short a distance. This time I took a few steps in its direction, and with the speed of a rabbit and the smoothness of running water it poured itself into a scrubby bunch of myrtle, but only when I had approached to within a few feet.

I then slowly walked toward my destination, but watched back for the snake to again erect itself. Imagine my surprise to see, instead, the grasses (about a foot high) being disturbed with that waving motion that only a snake in rapid transit can make and that disturbance headed directly toward me.

I then knew that I was being chased by the terrible black lash that, according to all tradition, would soon overtake me, wrap itself about my body and thrash me with its tail until I died in terrible agony. Upholding tradition, I should try my utmost to reach the nearest tree for salvation.

I did quicken my pace into a fast walk, noticing as I did that my curious friend also kept pace, occasionally rearing his head from the grass to sight his quarry. I then broke into a run — so did the snake; I suddenly stopped short — the snake did likewise. Quickly erecting its head from its running position to about two feet above the ground, he realized that I was too close for comfort. Into a clump of myrtle he dashed with me close on his trail. I was within about two feet of him before he again took to the open and this time he meant business; that is business at home, for if you want to see real speed just watch a five or six foot coachwhip when he is frightened. I watched for several minutes for him to again raise his head, but I have since learned that a coachwhip after once being frightened keeps his head down.

The above experience has been repeated only once, and both times in a pretty wild country. I believe from these experiences that neither of the two snakes that followed me had come in contact with man before and both were just downright curious. All others that I have seen have had their curiosity quieted and could, in all probability, tell from sad experience that the average man is not a very interesting animal with whom to play tag. I have run from many others, but could not get any action from them. Run toward any coachwhip and you get just a glimpse of a black streak through the grass. They will not fight unless cornered and in a pretty close corner at that.

But do not try to get friendly with one, for they *will* bite. I have taken as long as three or four minutes to get one to release my forefinger. Of course, the snake, not having fangs, cannot inflict much of a wound, but the tiny teeth are very sharp and the jaws strong.

So, don't doubt the person who says he has been chased by a coachwhip, but if he says he has actually been whipped — well, folks of that kind, are not nice to argue with anyway.

CHAPTER XI

Another Tarantula

Some time ago I became interested in the habits of a huge spider known throughout South Texas as the tarantula. In an article, appearing in *Field and Stream,* I dwelt on the fact that one certain individual allowed its cellmates all manner of liberties and accepted gross insults without retaliating with even a gesture of wrath. I write the following in apology for having had the temerity to set forth a single individual's behavior as symbolic to the habits of the entire species; I should have known better.

My second subject was captured in early spring and measured six inches spread out. After two months of solitary confinement sans food but well supplied with water, her abdomen shrunk to practically nothing; otherwise, she seemed in the best of health. With the apparent determination of a political prisoner or the delicacy of an avowed epicurean she spurned with disgust such food as was offered.

About this time I captured an eight-inch centipede and introduced it in the cage of the spider. I did not think there would be much of a fight and anticipated for the active centipede an easy victory — no, not victory, rather, an easy capture.

Clearly adhering to my anticipation the centipede began a hurried nervous reconnaissance of its new environment. Quietly and apparently disinterested, the tarantula crouched in its accustomed corner, nor did it move until actually touched by the antenna of the visitor. (The centipede depends almost entirely upon this appendage for guidance; it seems to be decidedly near-sighted.) Slow to resent these touches, the tarantula clumsily reared herself on her back legs and warded off the antennae with her two front feet. On each occasion the centipede stopped short as soon as its antennae warned it of the foe, and after a minute or two of hurried appraisal, continued the tour of inspection. Circling the cage several times it never failed to stop short and feel out for the spider; each time the same sparring took place.

Believing the situation would remain unchanged indefinitely, I proceeded to mix 'em up a bit. With a straw I prodded the visitor and the result was marvelous. It made the fatal mistake of blaming the insult upon its erstwhile phlegmatic host, the tarantula, and swung into action.

The skirmish ended as quickly as it had begun and the centipede retreated about ten inches, leaving a badly punctured but still defiant foe in her corner. I counted five distinct wounds on the body of the spider—three on her back and two in the fleshy parts of one foreleg. Drops of clear fluid exuded from these places and welled up as large as a pinhead. Apparently unconcerned with her wounds, the tarantula merely crouched back in a defensive attitude, holding her front feet in the air. Plainly in distress, the centipede was licking, or mouthing, a deep wound in his side.

Ten minutes elapsed before either of the combatants moved and then, as before, it was the centipede. But not as the aggressive, avid creature of a few minutes past. Seeming paralysis affected the ten forward segments of the body as well as the head and it propelled itself *backwards*! Blindly the strickened creature wove itself around the small enclosure in grotesque undulations, occasionally actually brushing against its antagonist, whose only response was an unhurried movement of the leg so touched.

Thirty minutes later the centipede was again in control of its being and there was another struggle with the tarantula. This time the advantage was entirely with the spider. After a second or two of action, too fast for the human eye, the ball uncoils and I see the tarantula gripping the tail of the centipede in grim earnest. The victim seems to be struggling to get away, not fighting back.

Slowly, but inexorably, the tarantula uses her front legs to hold back the two lance-like appendages protruding from the end of its victim. Then the mandibles are opened and with crushing force the fangs are embedded between the two darts. It is the "coup de grace."

I left the cage at this point and upon my return, an hour later, found that the spider had called off her hunger strike and had eaten two-thirds of the centipede and was still going strong. Eaten is not the proper word for there was left only a crushed mass of scales, shell, and legs at the side of the diner. Apparently, the tarantula, following the habits of her smaller kin, only drinks the juices or blood of its victims. Considerably heartened at the discovery of a palatable food for my captive I hastened to find more centipedes. Within the course of the following month she conquered and devoured three others, somewhat smaller.

I then withheld all chance of a banquet from her for the period of a month and introduced a half-grown mouse. Remembering the docility toward mice, sometimes suggesting downright affection that my first tarantula captive had displayed, I wished to test the temper or appetite of this one.

The mouse was introduced into the cage late one afternoon and an hour later, at dusk, I observed them. As on the other occasion — just two old pals, both huddled together in the darkest corner.

The next morning my inspection divulged no mouse. But its whereabouts was no mystery. Murder had been done! The abnormal obesity of the tarantula's abdomen pointed out the offender. She had gorged until her heavy belly left a tract in the fine sand on the floor of the cage.

In a corner was a mass of bones, hair, hide, and flesh—all that remained of her fellow captive.

The day following I caught another large centipede. Thinking to test the temper of my pet, when no victuals were in demand, I opened her cage door and dropped the centipede in upon the dormant creature. Her easy victories of the past, used as a criterion in the present instance, induced the action on my part. But I cannot excuse myself for forgetting her helplessness brought about by the feast of yesterday. The poor thing could hardly move, let alone fight.

The finish was quick — just one puncture of the balloon-like abdomen and the spider fell a helpless foe, in turn to be entirely devoured by the centipede.

(Reprinted with permission from *Field and Stream Magazine*)

CHAPTER XII

Tall Tales

There are many tall tales told about snakes. I hesitate to mention the less prevalent myths of snakes that I have heard for fear of insulting the intelligence of my readers, but I find it interesting to know that the following absurdities are commonly told as truths.

We have all heard that a dead snake with its stomach toward the sky forecasts rain, that the adder has a poisonous breath, and that all snakes are "slimy." But have you heard that a gun fired at a snake will never again direct a bullet on a true course? Or that a snake is so alert that a rifle or pistol bullet cannot be so directed that it will wound a snake other than in the head?

Sea serpents of gigantic proportions are ever being sighted; magazines are still entertaining the public with their stories of milk-drinking, bird-charming, broad-jumping snakes, and coach-whipping attacks. Recently, a magazine offered a prize for a motion picture film showing a mother snake in the act of swallowing her brood to protect them. The movies are supposed to prove without a doubt that a snake will use her body as a sanctuary for her offsprings. But will it prove the point? I question the validity of the experiment just as I question the following story told to me by a friend whose word in regard to other things I greatly respect but in this particular instance I challenge.

Wandering along the bank of a small stream, he surprised a large moccasin and her brood of twelve babies. Notwithstanding the fact that his foot had almost touched her, the mother ignored him as she hissingly warned her offsprings and then slightly rearing her head, she flung open her mouth and my amazed friend counted twelve little snakes dart from beneath her coils and pour themselves into the refuge. The drill began and ended in the fraction of a minute. As the last little snake disappeared within this peculiar sanctuary, the mother threw herself into a defensive position and silently awaited developments. As silently, the man watched for the second chapter of the story to unfold. In this he was disappointed. After a half-hour's vigilance, his patience gave way to curiosity and he shot her through the head with a small bore rifle. Then he cut off the snake's head, and picking her body up by the tail, he shook out the twelve little snakes who were none the worse for their experience.

You will find this story symbolic of all the stories told of a snake swallowing her young, the key lying not in the fact that a larger snake has been seen swallowing several smaller snakes but that the observer never actually assures himself of their egress by patiently watching until the larger snake voluntarily releases her brood. Since few of us know the anatomy of a snake well enough to pass on the likelihood of whether or not these little snakes are unborn offspring, recently swallowed food, or voluntary prisoners, I think it just as logical to suppose that a living frog or small animal rescued from the inside of a large snake might have entered for sanctuary purposes! Many of the stories told of larger snakes engulfing their young are found, but none are told of their resurrection.

It is not at all uncommon for a snake to disgorge a recently taken repast. This is generally done by most serpents either during the excitement of capture or immediately thereafter. Some time ago I was asked to examine a coral snake that had been caught by an engineering crew. It was brought to my office in a large bottle. On its arrival the bottle was opened and there appeared two snakes. One was a live coral and the other a garter snake — but dead. Investigation proved that only one snake had been captured, the coral. The men who had caught it were amazed, as the garter snake was a few inches longer than the coral. My conclusion that the garter snake was a disgorgement of a recent meal was unanimously protested.

I have noticed on numerous occasions this vulture-like trait of the snake. Shortly after feeding and if annoyed most all snakes will disgorge. There is a school of thought that the digestive fluids in a snake's stomach would soon kill a living organism including baby snakes. It is held that these fluids can dissolve the enamel of the tooth of a wild boar after a long period of digestion. This may be true, but I have reason to doubt this opinion.

As a boy, I distinctly remember the anguished cries of a frog coming from under a small log. A quick search beneath the log divulged a large water snake, but no frog. Realizing the situation, I decapitated the snake just in front of a slight protuberance on its neck. As the frog fell out and seemed to still be alive, I applied first aid treatment, water from my canteen. The frog revived with unpleasant memories and again began to bewail its fate in a series of frightened croaks. Soon it was again squatting on its haunches, and after a few invigorating punches with a small stick, it hopped gaining strength with confidence, and disappeared with anything but the hop of an invalid over the bank of a small creek. In all probability, its tale (if frogs tell tales) was received with the same credulity among its kind as the story Jonah insisted upon to the fishermen who found him wandering along the coast of the Mediterranean Sea.

True, this little adventure does not prove that a snake can or cannot hide twelve little snakes in its innards for the matter of a half-hour. The odds are great that a family of snakes once engulfed by a larger snake are merely that much breakfast, dinner, or supper as the hour dictates.

I am reminded of Aesop's fox who was reluctant to join the other subjects in paying their respects to his majesty, the Lion. The King of Beasts, as you recall, had commanded all of his vassals to visit him on his death bed in a narrow mouth cave. Reynard the Fox, after carefully studying the entrance to the cave was heard to remark over his shoulder as he slunk back into the jungle: "Excuse me, but I see all tracks leading into the cave, but none returning."

Another tale concerns seizing a snake by the tail and "snapping off its head." DON'T! Don't try it. It is generally considered a mark of courage by young boys. It is not to be disputed that a venomous serpent so treated has met its end at the hand of a very reckless and careless individual. That is if the snake has not first been beaten into a pulp before the tail is grasped. Surely, none of us can see anything so remarkable in the feat if practiced upon a dead snake. To "snap off the head" of a harmless snake is much less dangerous than to kill a small kitten or a small rodent in like manner.

To get hold of the snake's tail, let us observe the actions of any one of the pit vipers when suddenly disturbed. At the first sign of danger retreat being impossible, it will immediately throw itself into a defense coil with its vibrating tail either well inside the coil or as close to the outside walls of the coil as the motion of vibration allows. In this position I defy a human hand to seize the tail without receiving a wound from the fangs of the alert reptile.

If retreat seems possible to a nearby hole, vegetation cover, or a pool of water (all snakes are good swimmers), the snake will seek this refuge. Sometimes, as in the case of the rattlesnake, its attacking retreating motion strikes outward toward the danger and as it recovers into another coil it will have perceptively shortened the distance between its former position and its haven of refuge.

At other times it may move slowly but with dignified resentment, stopping only to threaten the least disturbance of its progress. Of course, if a place of safety is within a foot or two there is always the mad, frantic dash to safety. It often occurs that one may advance between a snake and its asylum. Under this condition the snake will invariably dart toward its shelter and if it must go between your feet to reach that point—go it will. Many stories dealing with attacking serpents are founded on such.

Now let us look into the many tales told that can easily be proved or disproved with a few actual experiments. Snakes do shed their skins at no certain interval, anywhere from six to eight weeks. The big snakes, pythons and boas, shed in patches as do the lizards, but the smaller snakes crawl out of their skins. Before a snake sheds, the epidermis hardens as the natural oil drys out; the colors fade and the iridescent glow, so prevalently found on most healthful snakes, dulls considerably. There is an interval of blindness, caused by the drying of the shell-like skin protecting the eyes. Then the snake regains its coloring and the milky blur that has blinded it disappears, leaving the sight unimpaired.

An oily secretion between the old and new skin is responsible for this dulling of the vision. The secretion is used as a lubricant. Now the act of actually removing the worn out skin is begun. Nosing its way to a rock, bush or tree, the snake rubs its head against the object until the old skin is gradually broken at the nose. Then, as the breach widens, it crawls out of the old epidermis. The skin turns inside out, exactly as the sleeve of the hurriedly removed coat of a careless schoolboy.

Many tales are told of a snake's love for music. These are as numerous as the stories dealing with an elephant's revenge after being tricked into accepting a piece of chewing tobacco. I have learned from elephant men that a chew of tobacco is considered a delicacy by the average elephant.

While it may be that the sound vibrations transmitted by a violin or flute may reach some sense of a snake it is doubtful if the snake would react in any manner different from other noises that are man-made. I suspect Kreisler himself would find a very unresponsive audience were his violin concertos played to a serpentarium. I do know that taped music has no effect whatsoever on the actions of many snakes. I have offered them programs ranging from Schubert's Serenade to the latest rock and roll, and their only response was the usual desire to explore a foreign environment.

Hundreds of these melodious minded snake stories have been told, but Hendrik de Leeuw, writing under the title of a Fellow Member of the American Geographic Society, brings to the world a most amazing story of India. According to this story, cobras were a positive danger to him because of his adeptness with his violin and their love of his music. He illustrates with an account of an evening's event.

Feeling musically inclined he was sitting on the veranda of his Indian bungalow and decided to break the solemn stillness of an Indian evening with a few selections. While playing, he turned and was horrified to see a large cobra within two feet of him. Not giving way to his intense desire to flee, as he realized that the music was all that was keeping the snake dormant, he continued to play while he softly slipped backward toward the door of his house.

For fear I shall be accused of exaggeration I shall quote the next few lines as it appeared in the September, 1929 issue of *Sportsman Digest:*

> ". . . . and so I played air after air of different character, and the effect was magical. The snake behaved like an ardent hot-blooded disciple of Paganini; every variation in the music, whether of volume or of tone, produced instantly a corresponding change in the attitude and conduct of the cobra. If I played a

> lively dance, it swayed its body sideways in quick time and yet in graceful curves. If I took up a soft, dreamy reverie, it instantly relapsed into sudden stillness as if lulled to sleep in that upright attitude. And when I started a grand soul-inspiring anthem its eyes glistened with increasing lustre; its hood expanded to the utmost; its body puffed out with pride and delight. And curious as it may seem, when I struck a number of false notes in rapid succession on purpose, the cobra winced and writhed in pain as if suddenly struck with a whip."

Such a story would be humorous if it were not written as a scientific article. As it stands, it is deplorable. A man with the right to use his membership title should be more careful with his writings than if writing strictly on his name alone. It is different with the Fakir of India. His is a vocation that needs must deal in superstition and fancy. Let him blow his pipes and charm his snakes and tourists with his tricks.

Since the serpent has no outward ear openings it still remains for the scientist to unravel the mystery surrounding its reception of sound waves. What organ and how does it warn the snake of the approach of danger? For warning it receives unquestionably. Never have I been able to surprise a snake and I have often tried. Time after time I have attempted to surprise one, but each attempt to do so has ended in only one way. I find my subject alertly eyeing my position, even though I have crept unseen behind the closely boarded side of its cage and peered at it through a tiny crack between the timbers. It is foolish for mankind to try to match his stealth against the active vigilance of so small and observant a wild creature as the snake.

If not sound or sight — then what? Radar?

Fabre, in his graphic account of the Great Monk Moth, proves without a doubt that these insects transmit information to each other although separated by vast distance without the aid of any sense that man can understand, while Ditmars positively declares that a snake hears with its tongue.

Generally advanced, but not universally accepted, is the theory that the tongue of a snake is so gifted, but a few well versed scholars believe that the body itself is sensitive to sound vibrations while others maintain their positions with one word that hides a multitude of sins — the sixth sense.

Before leaving these "tall tales" this one I consider a prize winner, told to me by a friend from deep East Texas in the "Big Thicket" area.

A boy in his early teens was brought to the hospital for treatment. Since the age of four he was the enigma of the country doctor in the piney woods community in which he lived. At about that age, it seems a very peculiar malady had affected his stomach which began as a slight swelling and gradually increased until the organ was swelled to incredulous proportions. Hookworm, a prevalent disease of the vicinity, was the first diagnosis, but after proven antidotes for this illness failed to relieve the abnormality, remedies for tapeworm and other parasitic worms were called upon with no success. Baffled, the good doctor sent the boy to the city for treatment.

There an X-ray revealed a large snake comfortably coiled within the walls of the stomach! An operation was greatly feared as the physician thought an undue disturbance might rile the guest and it would retaliate by biting the stomach of its host. (The usual conclusion that it was a poisonous snake had to be assumed.)

I am very sorry that I cannot finish the story. It is a good one, and in my opinion one that deserves an ending, but one that I have never heard completed. There is always a good explanation as to the snake's ingress — a snake egg having been swallowed — but so far as I can learn its egress is still upon the "knees of the gods" for it is the only "snake story" for which I have no ending.

CHAPTER XIII

The One That Got Away!

Carl Stimson made strong enemies and equally steadfast friends. One of these friends was Walter Davenport, editor of *Collier's Magazine.* They argued by letter about politics, business, contemporary living conditions, North vs. South, and were constantly teasing and plaguing each other with banter covering their deep appreciation of each other. Among their letters I found this literary gem to share with you:

September 25, 1954

"Dear Carl . . . .

"I am compelled at last to write to you because, my friend, I'm ashamed of you. Every day or two, it seems, anacondas, boa constrictors and pythons are escaping in Texas (Dallas chiefly) and defy recapture. I have a feeling that recapturing the creatures is half-hearted; none of you Texans care to invade the likely hideouts of the snakes.

"When I first heard of the python escaping in Dallas, I scoffed. In a day or so, I said to myself, Carl Stimson will get in his car in Houston, drive over to Dallas, and in language the creature can understand, lure him out of his tree, wrap him around his neck, and drive him back to the zoo. No trouble at all. In fact, Carl will probably drive the serpent down to that San Jacinto seafood restaurant as his guest, feed it a few tons of crabs, lobsters, clams, and mussels, and later carry him back to his cage.

"But no! The New York Times tells me the snake is still at large. In no paper do I find a hint of Carl Stimson going on a snake hunt. And to think of my friend sitting back in Houston permitting a mere python to flout the law, sneer at the police, and laugh at his faint-hearted hunters. Carl Stimson, the man I saw weeping in sympathy over a sick bushmaster, stroking the head of a 'fer de lance' and cramming his pockets with cobras, timber rattlesnakes, and cunning little coral snakes. As I say, I'm ashamed of you. I suspect sometimes that the python is not at large at all, but tucked away comfortably at your office in a desk drawer at Caroline and Rosalie where you frequently haul it out and play games with it.

"Let me hear from you, Carl."

WD

In reply, Carl wrote:

October 2, 1954

"Dear Walter,

"You have misjudged me. Fact of the matter is, I am playing a waiting game. Waiting until that little snake swims down the Trinity, into Galveston Bay, up Buffalo Bayou into Houston (see sketch enclosed). Then, and only then, will I do my stuff and Ft. Worth will have a hell of a time proving ownership. I am sure this will be Pete's route. Even pythons ultimately leave Dallas and come to Houston and while we do not go into hysterics about a little fellow like this — only 19 feet long — ours is 25 feet and weighs 247 pounds. (We weighed it about a year ago and it had not fed for 2 months).

"Incidentally, there was a newspaper article yesterday that said Pete (ain't that the dickens of a name for a python but, after all, Ft. Worth and Dallas have little imagination. We call our snake Kaa. Original, if Kipling had not written his *Jungle Book*.) was sighted in the Trinity River headed south. However that may be, it seems that Pete is trying his best to reach Houston and my scouts are all along the river to encourage him. I would say that he will get here within the next two or three days unless some damn fool fisherman intercepts him and uses him for bait.

"Kaa is getting along in age. My guess is about 30 years. He was only a small snake when we got him 17 years ago. Fact is, he was the same size as Pete then. He has developed a growth on his tail that worries me. I am afraid it is cancerous. We expect to cut off a little piece of it next week for a diagnosis. If malignant, an operation.

"As I suspected, Saturday evening just after our zoo had closed, the night watchman called me and told me that there was a small python trying to get into Kaa's cage. I went out there but it was such a scrawny, little specimen of snakehood that we did not want any part of it. Therefore, I chartered a plane and flew Pete back to his Forest Park Zoo home and turned him loose near his cage. Of course, all of this, Walter, is hush-hush, and I would hate for the real facts to come out.

"Well, enough of this for the time and may the Good Lord continue to like you, Walt."

(no signature)

CHAPTER XIV

Fact Not Fiction

1) More people are killed in the U.S. each year by cars than are killed by snakes in 800 years; i.e., 40,000 car deaths annually vs. 20-25 snakebite deaths yearly. [1]
2) Some 2,500 kinds of snakes are known to inhabit the earth.
3) Rattlesnakes are found only in the western hemisphere, none being found in the Old World or Far East.
4) Rattlesnakes are known in almost every state in the U.S. and the greatest number of species is found in the state of Arizona.
5) Texas has over 100 different kinds of snakes.
6) Rattlesnakes, copperheads, water moccasins, and coral snakes are all found in Texas. These are the four poisonous snakes in the U.S.
7) The Texas diamondback rattlesnake causes more deaths in the U.S. each year than all other poisonous snakes combined.
8) All the poisonous snakes in the U.S. can be identified by a large triangular head; the coral snake is a notable exception.
9) Coral snake antivenin serum is now made in this country; formerly, it was imported from Brazil.
10) No kind of native snake in the U.S. gets larger than nine feet.
11) Some snakes do lay eggs, but others hatch live young.
12) The period of incubation in snakes varies from 3 days to 4 months.
13) Pythons lay as many as 100 eggs.

14) Mother snakes do not swallow their young for their protection.
15) Snake venom is innocuous when taken internally by a healthy person.
16) Removing the fang does not entirely disarm a snake. The venom may be transferred into the wound caused by the small teeth behind the fang sheath; more important, the fangs will be replaced with new ones.
17) Snake poison is slightly heavier than water.
18) The tongue of a snake is not a stinger and is not used to poison prey nor to cause a wound. Its possible use is that of an antenna.
19) Snakes do not crawl faster than 15 miles per hour.
20) Snakes cannot stand extreme heat or cold because they are cold-blooded.
21) Most snakes will strike at anything that moves within one-half of the length of the snake, but a rattler will strike at its own length or even farther.
22) The facial pit of the rattlesnake helps to detect warm-blooded prey even in complete darkness.
23) Snakes do not chew their food. Their strong digestive juices dissolve almost everything eaten by them.
24) A snake's jaws are connected horizontally and vertically with ligaments. It appears to crawl over its food instead of pulling food into its mouth.
25) A snake's skin is very elastic. It may be stretched one-quarter over its normal length.
26) Snakes have been known to exist for more than three years without food.
27) Some snakes are beneficial to the farmer because they eat enormous quantities of destructive and disease-carrying rats and mice.
28) Snakes do not milk cows or even drink milk.[2]
29) Science notes no instance of a snake having swallowed a full-grown man, although such a tragedy is not only possible, but probable. There are reports on record of small children having been engulfed.
30) No snake has a poisonous spine on the end of its tail.

31) Boa constrictors are not the world's largest snake. Pythons grow to twice the length of boa constrictors. (31 to 32 feet)
32) Alligators do not live to be more than from 100 to 200 years old. Snakes live to be about 25 years old.
33) Snakes do sleep with their eyes open. Having transparent immovable eye-screens, it is impossible for them to close their eyes.
34) A snake has no outward ear openings, but has ear bones and is probably deaf to sound in the same sense as we know it.
35) A snake does not need to coil before it can inflict a wound.
36) The number of scales on a snake's stomach corresponds to the paired number of ribs the snake has.
37) About one snakebite in every fifteen is the result of people intentionally handling snakes.
38) Snakes are among the cleanest of all animals.
39) Snakes are not slimy.
40) Snakes are not blind just before they shed, yet they cannot see well.
41) Poisonous snakes have fangs and venom at birth.
42) The spreading adder is not poisonous and has no poisonous breath.
43) A dog, bitten many times by poisonous snakes, cannot transfer the venom by biting another animal, as in rabies.
44) The king snake is highly resistant to rattlesnake venom, but not immune.
45) The number of rattles forming the rattle do not tell a snake's age. A new segment is added with each shedding and many old segments are broken and or lost during the snake's lifetime. Few rattles exceed 15 inches. Longer sets are easily faked.
46) Snakes do bite under water.
47) Each and every bone of a snake's skeleton is not a poisonous dart.
48) Some snakes do hiss . . . loudly! Snakes have no

voice and cannot taste food.

49) There is no peculiar friendship between the owl, gopher, prairie dog and rattlesnake.
50) Contrary to the belief that a snake is so accurate in its aim that it will intercept with its head a bullet aimed at its body is the fact that a snake's aim is anything but perfect, due to the lack of coordination between the eye and the fang of a striking reptile.
51) Snakes do not always demand living food.
52) A horse hair immersed in rain water will always remain just that — a horse hair! Small hair-like creatures often found in stagnant water are only the parasitic worms of diseased grasshoppers.
53) Some lizards have no legs and look very much like snakes.
54) A snake cut into two or more pieces will not grow back together.
55) It is not true that a snake will not die until sundown if injured.
56) Snakes feel vibrations from the ground through their bellies.
57) Drinking whiskey does not help to cure snakebite. It is actually harmful to a snakebitten victim if used to excess as it increases circulation of the poison.
58) No snake forms a hoop of its body and in such a position rolls along the ground and chases people.
59) A snake will not "commit suicide" by plunging its fangs into its own body to escape a tormentor. Occasionally, in frantic agony, a snake will imbed its fangs in its own flesh, but this would be an accident.
60) Snakes cannot hypnotize other animals.
61) Pigs are not entirely immune to snake poison; their fatty tissue helps to absorb and to dispel much of the poison which is injected.
62) Except for the gila monster and the beaded lizard, there are no poisonous lizards in the U.S. They do not have to turn on their backs to inject their venoms.
63) Coachwhip snakes do not whip people with their tails.

64) A snake, thrown into a fire, is as incapable of showing its legs as a man would be of showing his wings in a like situation.
65) Snakes are probably the most misunderstood of all animals, but are to be less feared than disease-carrying flies and mosquitoes.
66) Most people bitten by snakes in the U.S. recover even without treatment, although they may be left with some physical impairment.
67) If you get snakebit, walk — DO NOT RUN — to the nearest medical aid.
68) Remember the first rule of prevention — LEAVE THEM ALONE!

[1] John E. Werler, Director of the Houston Zoological Gardens.
[2] John E. Werler, Director of the Houston Zoological Gardens, states that "in India, snakes have on occasion been induced to drink milk from a saucer."

\- - - - - -

Quoting from a letter dated 9/3/65 from Stimson to Don Micks of the Medical Branch of the University of Texas at Galveston:

> "Several weeks ago our Zoo Director was poisoned by an *atrox* on his little finger. Mr. Werler had been bitten twice before. On each occasion, he went into shock on the administration of antivenin. He was given 10 incisions, a slow drip of calcium glutanate, and iced for only 5 hours. He made a remarkably good recovery."

E. P. Haddon was present to record the details with his camera. The photos on the following pages show: 1) Rattlesnake ready to strike. 2) Werler using suction. 3) Stimson attending Werler at hospital. 4) Close-up of incisions and suction cups.

Photo 1: Courtesy of Ed Eakin, Eakin Publications.
Photos 2-4: Reprinted with permission of the author and photographer, E. P. Haddon from "When a Rattlesnake Bites," *Sports Afield Magazine,* November 1965.

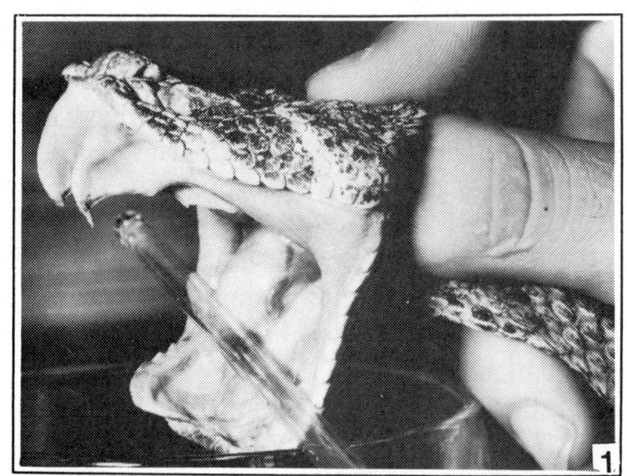

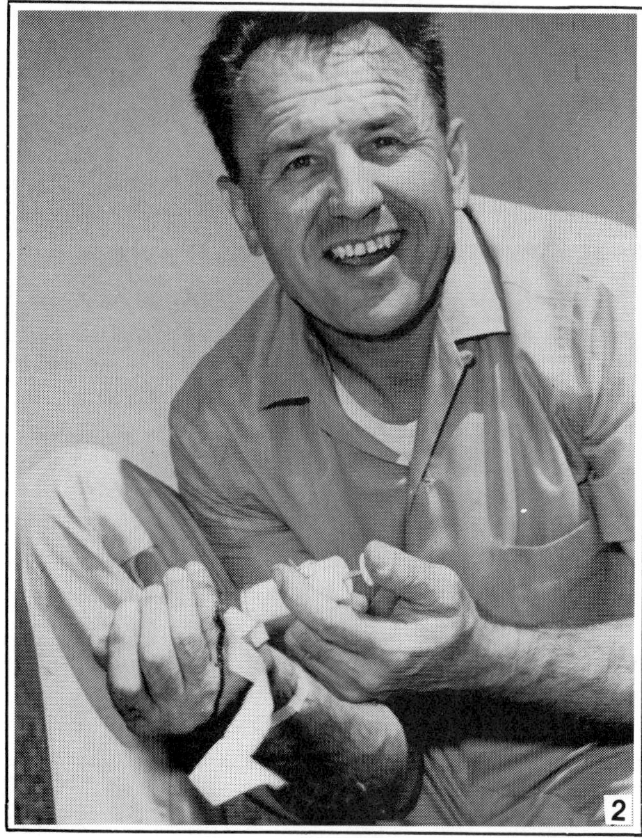

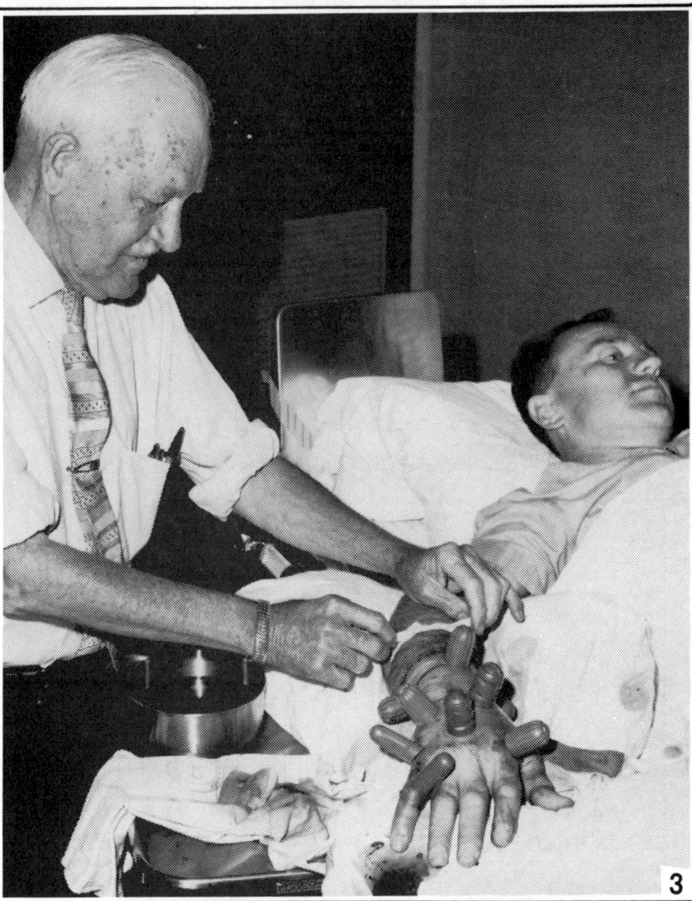

3

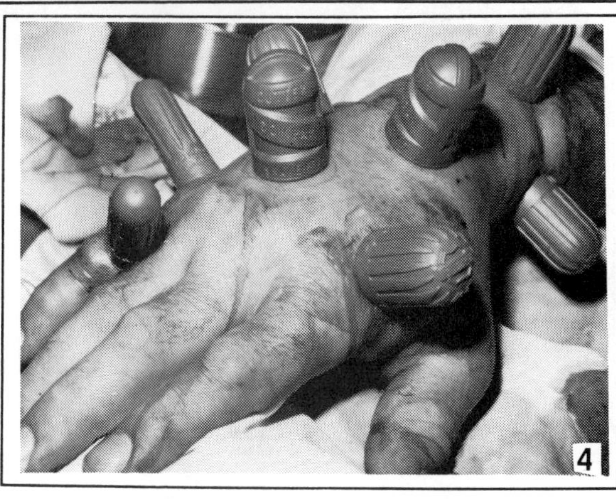

4

CANEBREAK RATTLER

ADULT WATER MOCCASIN

WESTERN GROUND RATTLER

CORAL SNAKE

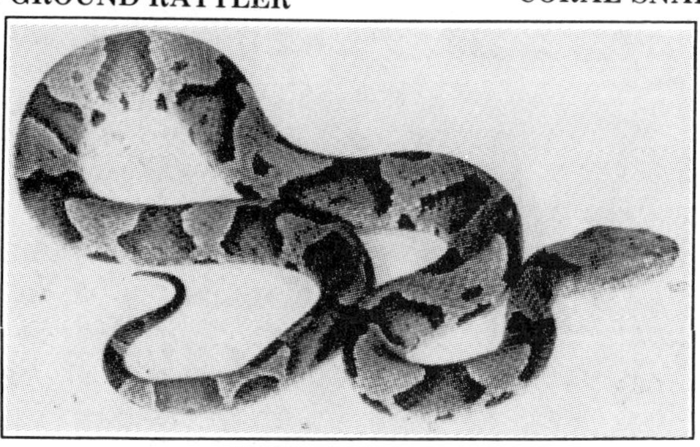

COPPERHEAD

Houston Zoo Photos, by Werler

Reprinted from the *Journal Of Occupational Medicine,* Vol. 2. No. 4 (April), 1960.

ADDENDUM

In checking through my Father's articles and notes, I found that in a reprint from the *Journal of Occupational Medicine,* Vol. 2, Number 4 (April) 1960 on page 167 that he and H.T. Engelhardt, M.D. (who coauthored the article) "agree with (F.S.) Shannon in regard to the danger of cryotherapy as advocated by (H.L.) Stahnke." (Danger of "trench foot.")

Not having inherited my Father's fondness and curiosity about snakes, I am unable to expand on this statement other than to observe that there seem to be many contradictions about treatment. (see Chapter III)

The Jesse Jones Medical Library in Houston was offered and accepted Stimson's file of over 800 case histories of snakebite, on which he had been consulted during a period of 20 years — from 1948 to 1968.

The following is a copy of a speech made by A.C. Stimson, when he was the Honorary Curator of Reptiles of the Museum of Natural History of Houston and the Houston Zoo, to the staff of the Veterans Administration Hospital on July 29, 1958.

SUGGESTED TREATMENT OF VENOMOUS ANIMAL POISONINGS

"Thank you, doctor. Your introduction has been most flattering. Doctors and Nurses of the Staff of the Veterans Hospital:

"After so complimentary an introduction, I am afraid you will be sadly disappointed in my paper. Please understand it comes not from a medical man but is only the suggestions of a self-taught herpetologist — a bit of knowledge that I have picked up in the past forty-five years in my rather close study in the field of reptile and insect life.

"I am, by vocation, a land surveyor. For lack of a

professional herpetologist and entomologist, until three years ago, I was asked to pinch-hit in that capacity for the Museum of Natural History and the Houston Zoo.

"Fortunately, in 1955, a real professional was retained by the zoo. He is Mr. John Werler, formerly Assistant Director of the Brackenridge Zoological Society of San Antonio and a nationally known student of reptiles, the author of many scientific papers and the discoverer of several new species of reptiles. I am very proud that I was a bit instrumental in bringing Mr. Werler to Houston as our General Curator. He has kindly consented to operate the visual aid for me tonight in the display of a few pictures that will be shown later.

"May I introduce him. Ladies and Gentlemen, John Werler.

"First, let me impress upon you the fact I know very little of the whys and wherefores of medicines and sera. By this I mean that although you doctors have taught me that calcium gluconate and other medicines and sera usually quiet a patient — why, I do not know, and I am entirely too old to learn. Therefore, please do not get too technical with me during the question period. However, Mr. Werler or some of you doctors may have the right answer to the questions you may ask that will be over my head.

"In 1949 I offered my services to the doctors and hospitals in identifying snakes that had accompanied a victim to their offices or to a hospital. I was allowed to stand by and to watch the treatments. Amazed at the variations and variabilities of these, I began intensive reading of the works of Drs. Dudley Jackson, Minton, Shannon, Stahnke, and other doctors, who had given much study to the subject. Due to the graciousness and courtesies of the doctors of this vicinity, I learned the best method of treatment used by one doctor and transmitted that information to the next one. In other words I consider myself merely a correlator transferring knowledge thus gained from one doctor to another. And, doctors and nurses, let me be emphatic on this point; I learn something every time I am called. Also, I always refuse to visit a victim of animal poisoning unless personally invited to do so by the physician in charge of the case.

"Let me return to the early variations of treatments I first witnessed. Some doctors applied warm packs, others cold; some used tight bandages to retard the swelling; surgery was performed in many cases sans a local anesthetic; and an antivenomous serum was the order of the day, only 10 cc antivenin being administered and no surgery. In those early days it was not unusual for me to be called after surgery, only to identify the cause of the trouble as a harmless snake. Aside from the coral snake and black widow bite, if the patient is in little pain and the swelling is slight and localized, chances are that the accident is not serious. Certainly, not so serious as to indicate an antivenomous serum. (see Fig. 1)

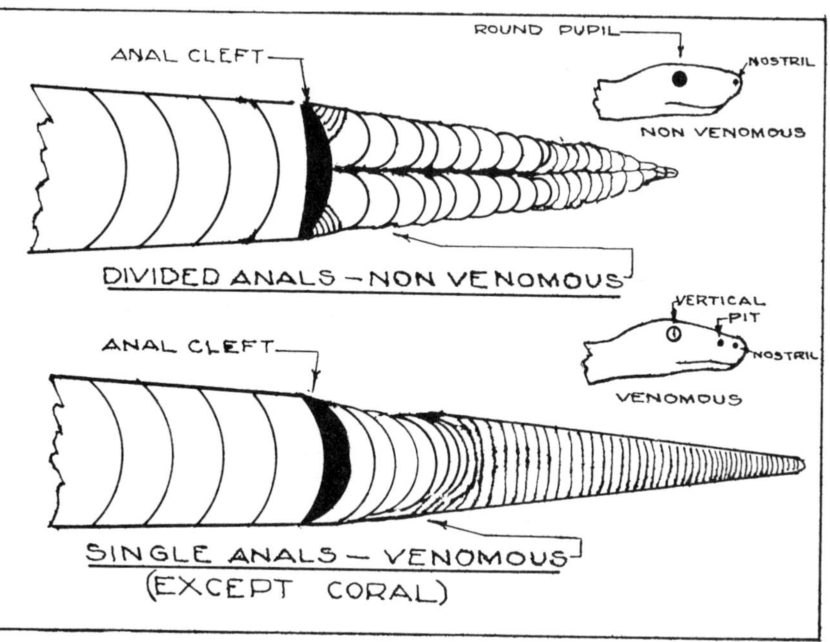

Figure 1

"Do not depend upon the skin or eye test. Even though the eye or skin tests are negative, I have seen some very bad reactions. While antivenin certainly has its place in the treatment of a serious snakebite case, it was proven secondary to incision and suction by Dr. Dudley Jackson many years ago. Personally, I consider the 10 cc contained in the Wyeth Company's ampule about like 300 units of penicillin—enough to cause a bad serum reaction but of little value toward neutralizing even an infinitestimally small amount of venom. If the accident is so serious as to demand an antivenomous serum, it should be administered in vast quantities; i.e., 40 to 120 cc intramuscularly at first, and in critical cases such as the bite of a large rattlesnake or moccasin or a wound on the face, thigh, neck, or trunk by any of our venomous snakes, then intravenously. Individual sensitivity plays no little part in the case of animal venoms and, incidentally, sera.

"Now, for my suggested treatment, and, remember, these are only suggestions, for what they are worth.

SNAKEBITE TREATMENT

1) "Use psychology especially on a neurotic patient. Tell him that there were only eighteen fatalities caused by snakebite in the whole of Texas in the past eight years according to the Mortality Reports of the State Health Department, against 38 deaths caused by wasps, bees, scorpions, and spiders; that of a total of more than 500 snakebites that I have seen in the past eight years, there have been no fatalities. While there is an occasional big rattler seen or captured in Harris County, I have seen only two cases. The big rattlesnakes caused all of the deaths reported with the exception of one suspect moccasin bite. On television four years ago, I said that I had heard of no fatal cases originating in Harris County in the past 45 years and asked my audience to cor-

rect me if they could cite me a death duly acknowledged by a death certificate signed by a licensed and reputable physician. I got many rumors, but investigation proved them just that — rumors.

2) "Usually a victim immediately constricts his arm so tightly that the venous return is badly retarded. This is quite dangerous, as snake venom is of such potency that it will not immediately mix with the blood stream . . . It backs into the lymph, is absorbed by that flow and, relatively speaking, flows slowly toward the heart. Release tight constrictor and replace with one loose enough to merely retard lymphatic flow. Release this two minutes out of every fifteen. Constrictor should be placed three inches above wound, toward the heart, and another above the elbow or knee.
3) "Sedate patient if in great pain or badly frightened. Give the heart a chance.
4) "Measure swelling two inches above wound. This should be repeated every hour, and time and measurements recorded.
5) "Check blood pressure and temperature at once and at hourly intervals thereafter.
6) "Check for blood stain in urine and type blood.

SURGERY

"Now for surgery. I have had reproductions of a drawing distributed among you for the purpose of making my meaning clear. (see Fig. 2)

1) "Under a local anesthetic, Novocaine or Procaine, incise across the fang punctures as shown in the drawing.

   "At the present time there is controversy [1] as to whether the fang punctures should be incised or the initial wound left untouched.

   "Minton writes that because of the spreading factor.

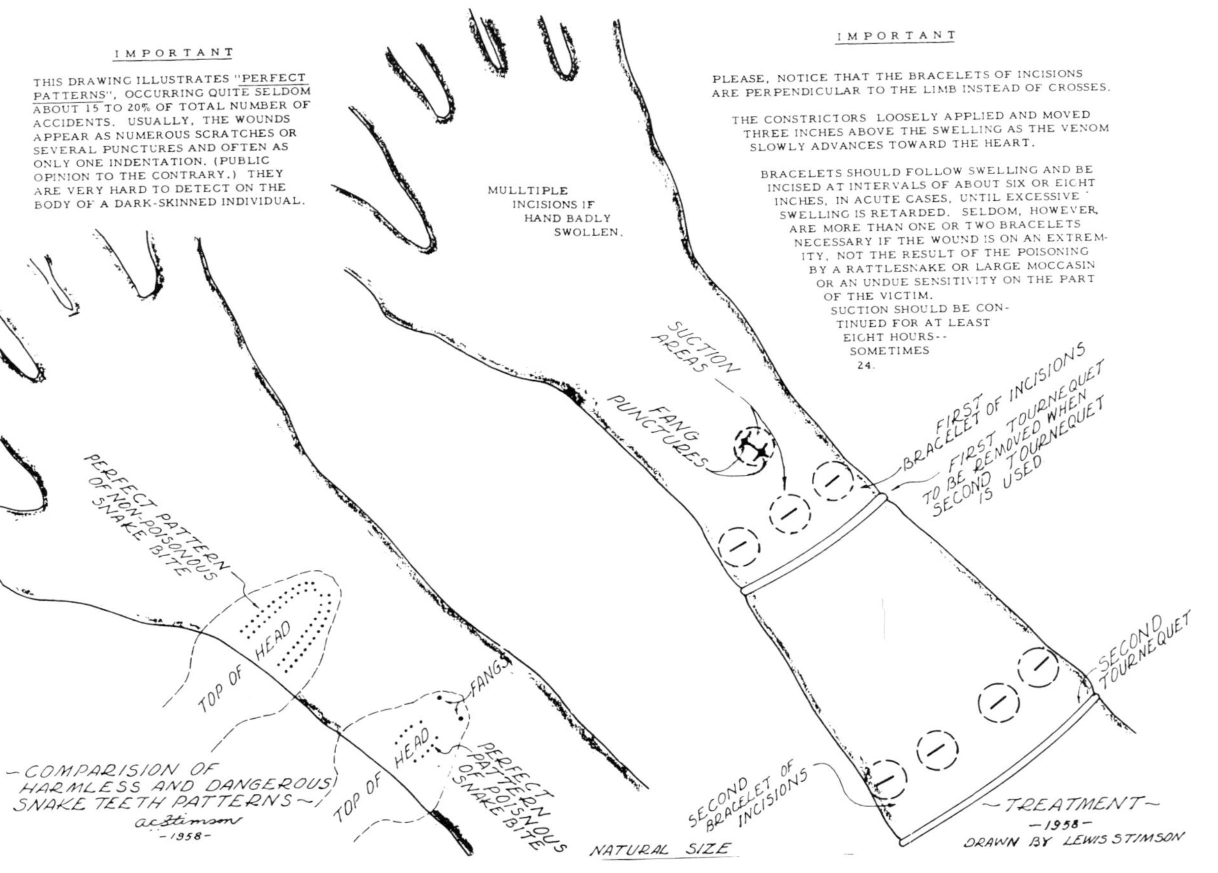
IMPORTANT
THIS DRAWING ILLUSTRATES "PERFECT PATTERNS", OCCURRING QUITE SELDOM ABOUT 15 TO 20% OF TOTAL NUMBER OF ACCIDENTS. USUALLY, THE WOUNDS APPEAR AS NUMEROUS SCRATCHES OR SEVERAL PUNCTURES AND OFTEN AS ONLY ONE INDENTATION. (PUBLIC OPINION TO THE CONTRARY.) THEY ARE VERY HARD TO DETECT ON THE BODY OF A DARK-SKINNED INDIVIDUAL.
MULLTIPLE INCISIONS IF HAND BADLY SWOLLEN.
IMPORTANT
PLEASE, NOTICE THAT THE BRACELETS OF INCISIONS ARE PERPENDICULAR TO THE LIMB INSTEAD OF CROSSES.
THE CONSTRICTORS LOOSELY APPLIED AND MOVED THREE INCHES ABOVE THE SWELLING AS THE VENOM SLOWLY ADVANCES TOWARD THE HEART.
BRACELETS SHOULD FOLLOW SWELLING AND BE INCISED AT INTERVALS OF ABOUT SIX OR EIGHT INCHES, IN ACUTE CASES, UNTIL EXCESSIVE SWELLING IS RETARDED. SELDOM, HOWEVER, ARE MORE THAN ONE OR TWO BRACELETS NECESSARY IF THE WOUND IS ON AN EXTREMITY, NOT THE RESULT OF THE POISONING BY A RATTLESNAKE OR LARGE MOCCASIN OR AN UNDUE SENSITIVITY ON THE PART OF THE VICTIM.
SUCTION SHOULD BE CONTINUED FOR AT LEAST EIGHT HOURS-- SOMETIMES 24.
SUCTION AREAS
FANG PUNCTURES
FIRST BRACELET OF INCISIONS
FIRST TOURNEQUET TO BE REMOVED WHEN SECOND TOURNEQUET IS USED
SECOND TOURNEQUET
SECOND BRACELET OF INCISIONS
~TREATMENT~
-1958-
DRAWN BY LEWIS STIMSON
NATURAL SIZE
PERFECT PATTERN OF NON-POISONOUS SNAKE BITE
TOP OF HEAD
FANGS
TOP OF HEAD
PERFECT PATTERN OF POISNOUS SNAKE BITE
~COMPARISION OF HARMLESS AND DANGEROUS SNAKE TEETH PATTERNS~
-1958-

the fang punctures should be left untouched, but I have a personal letter from Dr. Jackson that disagrees with this. Since I consider Jackson as being America's outstanding authority on the subject of treatment of snake poisoning, I suggest lancing across the punctures as shown on the drawing.

"Multiple incisions should be made across the 'puff iness' of the member, hand or foot, only deep enough (not over 1/8") to penetrate through the lymphatics and separators used to stimulate drainage. Contrary to general practice, I have found that much more drainage is had if the incisions are made perpendicular to the limb than the currently used crosses. (Linear cuts rather than cruciate ones.)

"Great care should be taken that the incisions are not longer than the diameter of the cup. Otherwise, all suction is lost. The Cutter Company is far superior to any other suction apparatus. Suction should be continued steadily (excepting when emptying cups) for two hours and the constricting bands in use, left on.

2) "If patient has shown no severe systemic reactions, remove constrictor but continue suction for at least eight hours, allowing rest periods of fifteen minutes per hour; i.e., suction cups on forty-five minutes and off fifteen. During fifteen minute rest intervals cover each incision with a warm saline pack laid across the incision to aid drainage. Bicarbonate of soda in large doses is advised.

3) "If, on the other hand, there are vomiting, respiratory difficulty, coma, hypertension, or great pain and advanced swelling use calcium gluconate, the drip method, and continue suction for as long as twenty-four hours if necessary. Under-treatment is decidedly more dangerous than over treatment. In other words treat each snakebite case as a serious one if the patient shows even the slightest systemic reaction.

4) "If the swelling increases greatly (say one-half inch) two inches above the wrist or ankle, bracelets of incisions are indicated. Move the lower constrictor three inches above the furthest point of swelling, incise and apply suction at equi-distant intervals around the member, being careful that the incisions are not so close together as to allow the suction cups to interfere with each other. Continue this procedure if the swelling still advances toward the heart, making additional bracelets three inches apart until the swelling has been retarded to only one-fourth inch, three inches above the last bracelet. Generally only two bracelets are necessary, but I have seen critical cases wherein an entire area was braceleted to the shoulder. The latter situation demands the use of antivenin in quantities I have previously mentioned.
5) "When the swelling has been retarded or has receded, go to refrigeration. Wrap the member in a towel containing cracked ice, not a cold water bottle, until his condition is satisfactory.

"During the entire treatment the patient should be closely observed for shock, especially a phlegmatic individual. The only cases of shock that I have seen were suffered by seemingly phlegmatic patients. Suppressed emotion? Every case is different. The doctor must observe this rule.

"For children under three years of age, this same treatment should be instituted, but with an additional treatment to quiet their tiny fears. Since the Veterans Hospital will have none or few of these, let me only mention that Dr. Guy Harrison of the Texas Children's Hospital uses an intravenous injection of Seconal, reenforced by rectal suppositories with great success.

"I am sorry that time will not permit me to speak of other venomous animal poisonings, and since it has sneaked up on me so rapidly, suppose we combine the question period with the showing of my pictures; some other venomous animals will appear, and your questions or criticisms will be more than welcomed as the pictures are run. Treatment of these and of the coral snake bite are entirely different. I would like to say a few words about the coral snake, time permitting."

To return to the article that appeared in the *Journal of Occupational Medicine,* let me quote from it about the coral snake. (pp 164-165)

> "The coral snake, a member of the Elapidae, secretes a venom in which a neurotoxin predominates. Death from such a snakebite is usually the result of bulbar paralysis.
>
> "Generally speaking, snake venom is composed of complex proteins which act as enzymes. Hyaluronidase is found in most venoms and is responsible for the quick spread of the venom along the lymphatics. Interestingly enough, the venom is rarely disseminated by the blood. The predominant venom of the pit vipers is a hemotoxin which causes a hemolysis of the erythrocytes and a disturbance in the clotting mechanism so that, at the site of the bite, there is ecchymosis, edema, and tissue destruction.
>
> "A venomous snakebite wound first appears as a small white wheal surrounding each puncture. The wheal usually progresses to red, and later may turn blue, green, or purple. Depending on the nature of the venom, edema is present in varying degrees at the site of the infection, and the patient complains almost immediately of an intense burning pain at the site of the bite.
>
> "At best snakebite treatment is heroic, and it would be interesting to learn of the number

of persons who have undergone this treatment after having been bitten by non-venomous snakes.

"It is known that snake envenomation usually results in a gradual increase in pain, while in other bites or stings there is usually a regression of pain with the passage of time. The exceptions are in bites of the black widow and its close relatives, the brown widow, and the red-legged widow.

"Most snakes, particularly the venomous ones, are chiefly active at night. Thus, there is increased danger of injury during the hours of darkness. It has been observed that the period between April and October is the time of greatest exposure. This period coincides with warmer weather and with increased outdoor activity such as hunting, farming, gardening, and vacationing."

Regarding medical treatment of coral snakebite, Stimson, in a letter to Ronald Barr, writes that he personally would suggest the "L-C" iced water treatment with no incisions or antivenin unless the serum manufactured in Brazil is obtainable.[2]

In conclusion, for the benefit of the reader who would like to pursue the treatment of snakebite in more detail, I have copied the references listed on page 168 of the *Journal of Occupational Medicine.* These are the authorities accepted by those who know this branch of medicine best.

[1] "Today's medical opinion suggests no incisions should be made if patient can reach physician within two hours," quoting John E. Werler, Director of the Houston Zoological Gardens.

[2] John E. Werler, Director of the Houston Zoological Gardens, informs me that coral snake antivenin serum is now made in this country and does not have to be imported.

REFERENCES

Allam, M.W.; Weiner, D.; and Lukens, F.D.W.: *Comparison of Cortisone and Antivenin in the Treatment of Crotaline Envenomation in Venoms.*

Andrews, E.H., and Pollard, C.P.: "Report of Snakebites in Florida and Treatment: Venoms and Antivenoms," *J. Florida M.A.* 40:388, 1953.

Jackson, D.: Personal Communication to the authors, Stimson and Engelhardt.

McCreary, T., and Wurzel, H.: "Poisonous Snakebites," *J.A.M.A.* 170:268, 1959.

Parrish, H.M.: "Deaths from Bites and Stings of Venomous Animals and Insects in the United States," *A.M.A. Arch. Medicine* 104:198, 1959.

Parrish, H.M.: Personal Communication to the authors, Stimson and Engelhardt.

Parrish, H.M.: "Poisonous Snakebites Resulting in Lack of Venom Poisoning," *Virginia M. Monthly* 86:396, 1959.

Parrish, H.M.: "The Nature of Poisonous Snakebites: Epidemiology, Diagnosis and Treatment," *Veterinary Medicine* 53:197, 1958.

Schwartzwelder, J.D.: "Snake Bite Accidents in Louisiana with Data on 306 Cases," *American Journal of Trop. Medicine* 30:575, 1950.

Shannon, F.A.: *Comments on the Treatment of Reptile Poisoning in Venoms,* Pub. 44, Washington, D.C., American Association for the Advancement of Science, 1956.

Stadelman, R.E.: "Poisoning Power of the Newborn Copperhead with Case Report," *Antivenin Institute America Bulletin* 2:67, 1928.

Stahnke, H.L.: *The Treatment of Venomous Bites and Stings,* Poisonous Animals Research Laboratory, Arizona State College, Flagstaff, Arizona, 1958.

Stimson, A.C.: "Venomous Animal Poisoning and Suggested Treatment," *Medical Records and Annuals,* 51:755, 1958.

HARRIS COUNTY MEDICAL SOCIETY
400 JESSE H. JONES LIBRARY BUILDING
TEXAS MEDICAL CENTER
HOUSTON, TEXAS 77025

November 9, 1964

Mr. A.C. Stimson
2119 Elmen Street
Houston, Texas 77019

Dear Mr. Stimson:

Thank you for your letter of October 29, 1964, advising of the information forwarded to Miss Parker of the Houston Academy of Medicine Library. May we express our appreciation to you for your help many times in the past to physicians. With kindest personal regards, I remain.

Very truly yours,

Bill E. Robertson
Executive Secretary

BER: ly

* Refers to his collection of snakebite medical reports from the major hospitals of Houston covering a period of over twenty years.

VENOMS BIBLIOGRAPHY

Alexander, F. "Death from Wasp Sting," *British Medical Journal,* 1: 1348, June 18, 1938.

Bellairs, Angus d'A. *The Life of the Reptile.* London: Weidenfeld and Nicolson, 2 v., 1969.

Bellairs, Angus d'A. and Attridge, J. *Reptiles.* London: Hutchinson, 1975.

Bellairs, Angus d'A. and Carrington, Richard. *Reptiles.* N.Y.: American Elsevier Pub. Co., 1966.

Brown, John H. *Toxicology and Pharmacology of Venoms from Poisonous Snakes.* Springfield, Ill.: Thomas Pub. Co., 1973.

Bucherl, W.; Buckley, E.; and Deulofeu, V. (editors) *Venomous Animals and Their Venoms.* N.Y.: Academic Press, 1968.

Caras, Roger A. *Venomous Animals of the World.* Englewood Cliffs, N.J.: Prentice-Hall, Inc. 1974.

Caras, Roger A. *The Venomous Animals.* N.Y.: Barre/Westover Books, distributed by Crown Pub. Co., 1974.

Calaresu, I. "Poisoning Caused by Spider Bite," *Minerva Medicine,* 50: 3819-3825, November 24, 1959. In Italian.

Chiggers — How to Fight Them. U.S. Department of Agriculture Leaflet 403.

Cooperative Economic Insect Report. Plant Pest Control Division; Agricultural Research Service; U.S. Department of Agriculture, vol. 9, number 13, March 27, 1959.

Courter, E.D. *Bat Rabies.* Rabies Health Report. 69: 9-16, 1954.

Ditmars, Raymond Lee. *Reptiles of the World.* (revised edition) Macmillan. 1933.

Ditmars, Raymond Lee. *A Field Book of N. American Snakes.* N.Y.: Doubleday-Doran, 1939.

Ditmars, Raymond Lee. *The Reptiles of N. America.* N.Y.; Doubleday-Doran, 1951.

Ditmars, Raymond Lee. *Snakes of the World.* N.Y.: Macmillan, rev. 1970.

Eisner, Thomas. "Defensive Spray of a Phasmid Insect," *Science,* vol. 148, number 3672:966-968, May 14, 1965.

Fabre, Jean Henri Casimir. *Insect World.* Dodd Pub. Co 1949. 333 pp. (Comments by E.W. Teale.)

"Facts About the Imported Fire Ant," *Highlights of Agricultural Research,* vol. 5, number 4, winter 1958.

Facts About the Imported Fire Ant Eradication Program. Agricultural Research Service; U.S. Department of Agriculture, April 1958.

Favorite, F.G. "The Imported Fire Ant," *Public Health Report,* vol. 73: 445-448, 1958.

Fire Ant Eradication Program and How It Affects Wildlife. Columbia, S.C.: Southern Association Game and Fish Commission, 1958.

Frazier, C.A. "Reactions to Stinging Insects and Treatment," *General Practitioner,* 22:96-100, July 1960.

Garner, C.F. *Carpenter Ants.* Pub. by Texas A&M University, n.d.

Goldstein, N.P. "Neuritis Occurring after Insect Stings," *Journal of the American Medical Association,* 173:1727-1730, August 1960.

Halstead, B.W. *Dangerous Marine Animals.* Centreville, Md: Cornell Maritime Press, 2nd Edition, 1980.

Halstead, B.W. *Poisonous and Venomous Marine Animals of the World.* Washington, D.C.: Government Printing Office, 3 vol., 1965-1970. Revised Edition Princeton, N.J.: Darwin Press, 1978.

Harmon, R.W. and Pollard, C.B. *Bibliography of Animal Venoms.* Gainesville: University of Florida Press, 1948.

Hocking, B. "Northern Biting Flies," *Annual Review of Entomology,* 5:135-152, 1960.

Hudson, B.W., Feingold, B.F., and Kartman, L. "Allergy to Flea Bites," *Experimental Parasitology,* 9:264-270, June 1960.

How to Control the Imported Fire Ant. Texas Agricultural Extension Service; College Station, Texas, n.d.

Imported Fire Ant and How to Control It. U.S. Department of Agriculture, Leaflet 350.

"Insect Stings," *British Medical Journal,* Number 5149:417-418, September, 1959.

Jackson, Dudley, M.D. "Treatment of Snake Bite," *Southern Medical Journal,* 22:605-608, 1929.

Klauber, Lawrence Monroe. *Rattlesnakes: Their Habits, Life Histories, and Influence on Mankind.* Berkley: Pub. for the Zoological Society of San Diego by the University of California Press, 1972. 12th Ed.

Klotz, Alexander B. *Metamorphosis.* Garden City, N.Y.: Pub. by Nelson Doubleday, Inc. for the National Audubon Society, 1955.

Kuna, J. "Death in a Hypersensitive Person Due to Bee Sting," *Zentralblatt fuer allgemeine Pathologie und Pathologische Anatomie,* v. 100:461-463, April 26, 1960. In German.

Mallis, A. "Bed Bugs and Other Bugs," *Handbook of Pest Control.* New York: MacNair-Dorland Co. 392-418, 1960.

Micks, Don W., M.D. "Insects and Other Arthopods of Medical Importance in Texas," *Texas Report on Biology and Medicine,* volume 18, number 4:624-635, winter 1960.

Minton, Sherman A. Jr., M.D. *Some Health Problems for the Medical Zoologist in the "Big Bend" Country.* Department of Microbiology, Indiana University School of Medicine, n.d.

Minton, Sherman A. Jr., M.D. *Venomous Animals, Spiders, and Insects.* 1959.

Minton, Sherman A. Jr., M.D. and Minton, Madge Rutherford. *Venomous Reptiles.* New York: Scribners Pub. Co., 1969.

Minton, Sherman A. Jr., M.D. and Minton, Madge Rutherford. *Giant Reptiles.* New York: Scribners Pub. Co., 1973.

Mueller, H.L. "Further Experiences with Severe Allergic Reactions to Insect Stings," *New England Journal of Medicine,* 261:374-377, August 20, 1959.

Mueller, H.L. "Serious Allergic Reactions to Insect Stings," *American Journal of Nursing,* 60:110-112, August 1960.

Mueller, H.L. "Yellow Jacket Sting," *Journal of the American Medical Association,* 173:1165, 1960.

Munwald, J., Chadha, M.S., Hurst, J.J., Eisner, T., *Defense Mechanisms of Arthropods — IX. Anisomorphal, the Secretion of a Phasmid Insect.* New York: Pergemon Press, 1962.

Observations on the Biology of the Imported Fire Ant. Agricultural Research Service; U.S. Department of Agriculture. Number ARS-33-49, August 1958.

Parker, H.W. and Grandison, A.G.C. *Snakes, A Natural History.* Ithaca and London: Cornell University Press; British Museum of Natural History, 2nd edition, 1977.

Parrish, Henry M. *Analysis of 460 Fatalities from Venomous Animals in the United States.* Division of General Medical Science, Public Health Service, PHS research grant GM10426-01, n.d.

Parrish, Henry M. and Donovan, Louis P. "Bites by Poisonous Snakes in South Carolina," *South Carolina Medical Association Journal,* 60:33-40, February 1964. Reprint.

Parrish, Henry M. and Donovan, Louis P. "Facts About Snakebites in Alabama," *Medical Association of Alabama Journal,* v. 33, number 10: 297-305, April 1964. Reprint.

Parrish, Henry M. and Donovan, Louis P. "Incidence of Poisonous Snakebites in Mississippi," *Journal of the Mississippi State Medical Association,* vol. V, number 6:222-228, June 1964. Reprint.

Parrish, Henry M. and Donovan, Louis P. "On Poisonous Snakes in Georgia," *Journal of the Medical Association of Georgia,* v. 53, number 7, July 1964. Reprint.

Parrish, Henry M. and Donovan, Louis P. "Ophidiases in Oklahoma," *Oklahoma State Medical Association Journal,* 254-260, June 1964.

Parrish, Henry M. "The Poisonous Snake Bite Problem in Florida," *Quarterly Journal of the Florida Academy of Science,* v. 20(3), 1957. Reprint.

Parrish, Henry M. "Poisonous Snakebites in North Carolina," *North Carolina Medical Journal,* vol. 25, number 3, March 1964. Reprint.

Parrish, Henry M. and Donovan, Louis P. "Snakebite Accidents in Kentucky," *Kentucky State Medical Association Journal,* April 1964. Reprint.

Parrish, Henry M. *Poisonous Snakebites in the United States.* New York: Vantage Press. 1st Edition, 1980.

Parrish, Henry M. "Survey of Snakebites in West Virginia," *West Virginia Medical Journal,* vol. 60, number 6:143-149, June 1964. Reprint.

Parrish, Henry and Donovan, Louis P. "Venomous Snakebites in Tennessee," *Tennessee Medical Association Journal,* vol. 57, number 4:141-146, April 1964. Reprint.

Periodical Cicada. (The 17-year locust) Washington, D.C.: U.S. Department of Agriculture. Leaflet 340.

Pomerantz, Charles. "Anthropods and Psychic Disturbances," *Entomological Society of America Journal,* vol. 5, number 2:65-67, June 1959. Reprint.

Porter, Kenneth R. *Herpetology.* Philadelphia and London: Saunders, 1972.

Pope, Clifford H. and Perkins, Marlin R. "Difference in the Patterns of Bites of Venomous and Harmless Snakes," *Arch. Surgery.* vol. 49:331-396, 1944.

Pope, Clifford. *Reptile World.* New York: Knopf Pub. Co., 1955.

Pope, Clifford. *Snakes Alive.* New York: Viking Press, 1937.

Russell, Findlay E. and Harreveld, A. Van. "Cardiovascular Effects of the Venom of the Round Stingray Urobatis Halleri," *Venoms.* American Association for the Advancement of Science. n.d. Reprint.

Russell, Findlay E. and Long, Truman E. *Effects of Venoms on Neuromuscular Transmission.* Laboratory of Neurological Research, College of Medical Evangelists, Los Angeles County Hospital, Los Angeles, California.

Russell, Findlay E., M.D.; Fairchild, M. David, M.S.; Michaelson, Joseph, Ph.D. "Some Properties of the Venom of the Stingray," *Medical Arts and Science,* vol. XII, number 2. Second Quarter. 1958. Reprint.

Russell, Findlay. "The Stingray," *Engineering and Science,* vol. XVII, number 3:15-18, 1953.

Russell, Findlay E., M.D. *Stingray Injuries.* Public Health Report, Public Health Service, U.S. Department of Health and Welfare, vol. 74, number 10:855-859, October 1959.

Russell, Findlay E. *Snake Venom Poisoning.* N.Y.: Lippincott Pub., 1980.

Russell, Findlay E. *Marine Toxins and Venomous and Poisonous Marine Animals.* Neptune City, N.J.: T.F.H. Publications, 1971.

Russell, Findlay E., M.D.; Panos, Theo C., M.D.; Kang, Louis W., B.A.; Warner, Allan, M.D.; and Colket, Trisham C. III., M.D. *Studies of the Mechanism of Death from Stingray Venom — A Report of Two Fatal Cases.* Laboratory of Neurological Research, College of Medical Evangelists, Los Angeles County Hospital, Los Angeles, California.

Schenken, J.R.; Tamisica, J.; and Winter, F.O. "Hypersensitivity to Bee Sting," *American Journal of Clinical Pathology,* 23:1216, 1953.

Schloch, J. "Insect Stings and their Treatment," *Praxis,* vol. 49:401-405, April 21, 1960.

Schmidt, Karl Patterson and Inger, Robert F. *Reptiles of the World.* 1957.

Scott, Harold George, Ph.D. *Envenomization.* U.S. Department of Health, Education, and Welfare, Public Health Service, Communicable Disease Center, Atlanta, Georgia, 1961.

Smith, Francis D., M.D.; Eaton, William B., M.D; Miller, Norman G., Ph.D.; Carnayzo, S.J., M.D. "Insect Bites by Avilus Cristalus, A North American Reduviid," *American Medical Association Archives of Dermatology,* vol. 77; 324-330, March 1958.

Snake Venoms (Handbook of Experimental Pharmocology). New York: Spinger-Berlag Pub. Co., vol. 52, 1979. (edited by Chen-Yuan Lee)

Stahnke, Herbert L., Ph.D. *Scorpions.* Arizona State College Bulletin, Tempe, Arizona, 1949.

Stahnke, Herbert L., Ph.D. *The Treatment of Venomous Bites and Stings.* Flagstaff, Az.: Poisonous Animals Research Laboratory, Arizona State College, 1958.

Suranepoel, A. "Tick Paralysis," *South Africa Medical Journal,* vol. 33:909-911, October 1959.

Susa, M. "Biology of Chiggers," *Annual Review of Entomology,* vol. 6:221-224, 1961.

Swinny, Boen. *Severe Reactions from Insect Stings.* Paper read before Section of Medicine, State Medical Association of Texas Annual Session, Ft. Worth, May 2, 1950.

Swoop and Grab. *Venoms.* 1956.

Thomas, J.W. "Insect Sting and Bite Reactions: Their Seriousness and Management," *Virginia Medical Monthly,* 86:617-619, November 1959.

Thorp, R.W. and Woodson, W.D. *Black Widow: America's Most*

Poisonous Spider. Chapel Hill: University of North Carolina Press, 222 pp., 1945.

Tu, Anthony T. *Venoms: Chemistry and Molecular Biology.* New York: Wiley Pub. Co., 1977.

Venoms. American Association for the Advancement of Science, Publication No. 44, XII, 467 pp. 1956.

Wasps — How to Control Them. U.S. Department of Agriculture. Leaflet 365.

Werler, John E. *Poisonous Snakes of Texas and First Aid Treatment of Their Bites.* Texas Game, Fish, and Oyster Commission, Bulletin No. 31:1-35, 1950.

Werler, John E. *Poisonous Snakes of Texas and First Aid Treatment of Their Bites.* Austin: Texas Parks and Wildlife Department, c 1964, revised edition of Bulletin No. 31 (1950) in 1978.

Zin and Smith, H. *Reptiles and Amphibians.* New York: Golden Press, 1956.

INDEX

Albalos, J.W., M.D., 22
allergy to serum, 24
Amaral, Afranio, M.D., 32
anaconda, 32, 34
antitoxin
    see serum
antivenin
    see serum
arachnids, 3
    see also black widow spider
    see also scorpion
Arizona snakes, 5
Arizona king snake, 16
ash worm, 4
asp, 4

Barbour, 14
Barr, Ronald, 92
Baylor, Tom, 33, 36
black snake, 48
black widow spider, 3-4, 25-26, 92
Blanchard, M.D., 8
blindness of snakes, 67
boa-constrictor, 40, 73-74, 77
    see also python
Brackenridge Zoological Society of San Antonio, 84
brood swallowing, 66-67

camouflage, 10, 12
cancer treatment, 19
cannibal snakes, 6
caterpillar, 4
centipede, 4, 61-64
"charming", 38-42
chicken snake, 41, 48
coachwhip, 6, 58-60, 77
cobra, 17, 43, 49, 70
cobra venom *(Cobroxin)*, 19
coloring, 69
    see also camouflage
copperhead, 1-3, 6, 11-13, 75
coral snake, 1-3, 7, 10, 14-19, 25, 75, 91-92
    description, 15
cortisone, 25
"cotton mouth" moccasin, 11-12
Crimmins, Colonel C.L., 14-15
cryotherapy, 21-23
Cutter Company, 89

dangerous snakes
    see poisonous snakes
Davenport, Walter, 73-74
deafness of snakes, 71, 77
de Leeuw, Hendrik, 70
diamond back rattlesnake, 24
    see also rattlesnake
Ditmars, Raymond Lee, M.D., 14, 49, 72

Eakin, Ed, 79-80
Englehardt, H.T., M.D., 83
engulfing, 31, 34, 67, 76

Fabre, Jean Henri, 71
feeding habits of snakes, 13, 31-37, 77
    see engulfing
    see disgorgement
feigning death
    see spreading adder
"fer de lance", 43
Field & Stream, 61
Forest Park Zoo, 74

gaboon viper, 43
gangrene, 23, 83
garter snake, 67

gila monster, 77
see also lizards
Goldsmith, 56
ground rattlesnake, 1, 9-11
see also rattlesnake

Haddon, E.P., cover, ix, 79-81
haemolytic reactions, 20
harmless snakes, 6-7, 16-17, 27, 92
Harris County Medical Society, 94
Harrison, Guy, M.D., 90
hearing of snakes, 71, 77
hissing of snakes, 77
Hofferbert, Louis, v
hognosed snake, 13
hoop snake, 52-54
Hornaday, ____, M.D., 14
Houston Lighting & Power Co., vi
Houston Post, 14
Houston Zoological Gardens, viii, 33
Hunt, Judge Wilmer, viii

identification of snakes, 6-18
indigo snake, 48
insects experiments, 61-64
insect stings, 3-5
see also asp
see also black widow spider
see also scorpion
see also tarantula

Jackson, Dudley, M.D., 14, 86
Jesse Jones medical Library, 83
Journal of Occupational Medicine, 9, 92

Kaa, 33, 36-37, 73-74
king snake, viii, 8, 77
see also Arizona king snake

L-C snakebite treatment, 21-23, 83
leukemia treatment, 19
lizards
see poisonous lizards
Loch Ness Sea Serpent, 56
locomotion of snakes, 17
locusts, 13

McClung, 32
McWhinney, 14
Methodist Hospital, The, vii
Mexican milk snake, 16
Micks, Don, M.D., 79
Midgard, 55
milk snake, 48-51
mimic snakes
see spreading adder
Minton, Sherman, M.D., 87
moccasin, 1, 3, 6, 10-12, 75
see also "cotton mouth"
see also "rattlesnake moccasin"
mongoose, 3
Museum of Natural Science, v, 83

neurotoxic reactions, 20
non-allergic snake serum, iv, viii, 19

Parrish, Henry, M.D., 14
pigmy rattler, 1, 9-11
see also rattlesnake
"Pit Viper", 7, 17
poisonous lizards, 77

poisonous snakes, Africa
- boa-constrictor 40, 73-74, 77
- gaboon viper, 43

poisonous snakes, India
- cobra, 17, 43, 49, 70

poisonous snakes, N. America, 6-18, 75-77
- copperhead, 1-3, 6, 11-13, 75
- coral, 1-3, 7, 10, 14-19, 25, 75, 91-92
- moccasin, 1, 3, 6, 10-12, 75
- rattlesnake, 1, 4-6, 8-9, 17, 19, 24, 56, 75
  - ground rattler, 1, 9-10
  - pigmy rattler, 1, 9-10

poisonous snakes, S. America
- boa constgrictor, 31, 34, 35
- "fer de lance", 43
- python, 31-35

Pope, Clifford, 35
puss worm, 4
python, 32, 36, 75, 77
- see also boa constrictor
- see also Kaa

racer snake, 6
rattlesnake, 1, 4-6, 8-9, 17, 19, 24, 56, 75
- Arizona, 75
- Florida, 56
- Texas, 75
- see also ground rattler
- see also mimic rattler
- see also pigmy rattler

rattlesnake moccasin, 9, 12
reproduction of snakes, 17, 75
Russell, Findlay E., M.D., 5, 14

scorpion, 4, 22
Scott, Major, 14
sea serpent, 55-57, 65
serpents in religion, 55
serum
- see snakebite serum

Shannon, Fred, M.D., 1, 5, 83
shedding skin, 17, 69, 76
Sherman, Carl B., vi
sizes of snakes, 31-33, 36, 56
Slinky, 35
snake experiments, 38-51, 58-64
snake stories, 48-60, 65-72
snake venom
- see venom

snakebite, vi, 1
- deaths, 13-14, 75, 86, 91
- gangrene, 20, 22-23
- handling, 1-2, 19, 77
- immunization of mongoose, 3
- prevention, 1-5
- reports, x
- serum, 21, 24-25, 85
  - allergic (toxic) reactions, 2, 24-25
  - non-allergic, iv, viii, 19
  - coral snake serum, 75
- symptoms, 12, 19, 26, 89-91
  - *haemolytic,* 20
  - *neurotoxic,* 20, 91
- treatment, 19-29
  - "backwoods surgery", 20
  - hospital surgery, 87-90
    - Stimson, 82-93, 87-90
  - L-C (Ligature-Cryotherapy), 20-23
- variable factors, 13, 25, 86
- see also venom

snakes
- age, 77
- albinism, 15
- beneficial, 76
- brood swallowing, 66-67
- camouflage, 10, 12
- "charming", 38-42
- deafness, 71, 77
- disgorgement, 35, 66-67
- "engulfing", 31, 34, 67, 76

feeding habits, 13, 31-37, 77
identification of, 6-18
hypnotism, 77
locomotion of, 17
melanism, 15
mimics, 15
physiological characteristics, 16-18
anals, 85
belly, 17
cold-blooded, 76
ear openings, 71, 77
eyes, 17, 77
facial pit, 75
fangs, 16, 27, 76
hissing, 77
jaws, 17, 34, 76
locomotion, 17
rattle, 8-10, 77
sense of smell, 17
skin, 17, 69, 76
teeth, 16, 76
tongue, 17, 72, 76
see also sizes
see also venom
reproduction of eggs, 17, 75
sizes, 31-33, 36, 56
striking, 17
venom, viii, 2-3, 17, 20
see also harmless snakes
see also poisonous snakes
see also serpents
spiders
see black widow
see tarantula
Sports Afield Magazine, 79
Sportsman's Digest, 70
spreading adder, 10
feigning death, 43-47, 77
Springer, G.B., vi
Stahnke, Herbert L., M.D., 21-23, 29-30, 83
Stimson, Arthur Carl, iv-ix
animal experiments
boa constrictor, 38-42
coachwhip, 58-60
milk snake, 48-51
spreading adder, 43-47
tarantula, 61-64
letter to W. Davenport, 73-74
non-allergic serum experiments, 19
snakebite treatment, 79, 81, 83-92
Stimson, Irene Gawley, ix
Stimson, J. Lewis, ix, 88

tarantula, 4-5, 61-64
Texas Crippled Children's Hospital, 90
Tobias, Ben, vii
Tucker, E.J., M.D., vi

venom, 2-3, 8-9, 13, 19, 23, 25, 27-28, 76, 92
haemolytic, 20
neurotoxic, 20
venomous snakes
see poisonous snakes
venomous animals, 57
Veterans Administration Hospital, 83

water moccasin
see moccasin
water snake, 31, 34, 54
see also anaconda
Werler, John E., viii-ix, 29, 79, 80-82, 84, 92
Willis, 33
Wright, Ruth Haddon, ix